S0-BAL-556

DAYLILIES

I. The Mikado Daylily. *Courtesy of The New York Botanical Garden Library.*

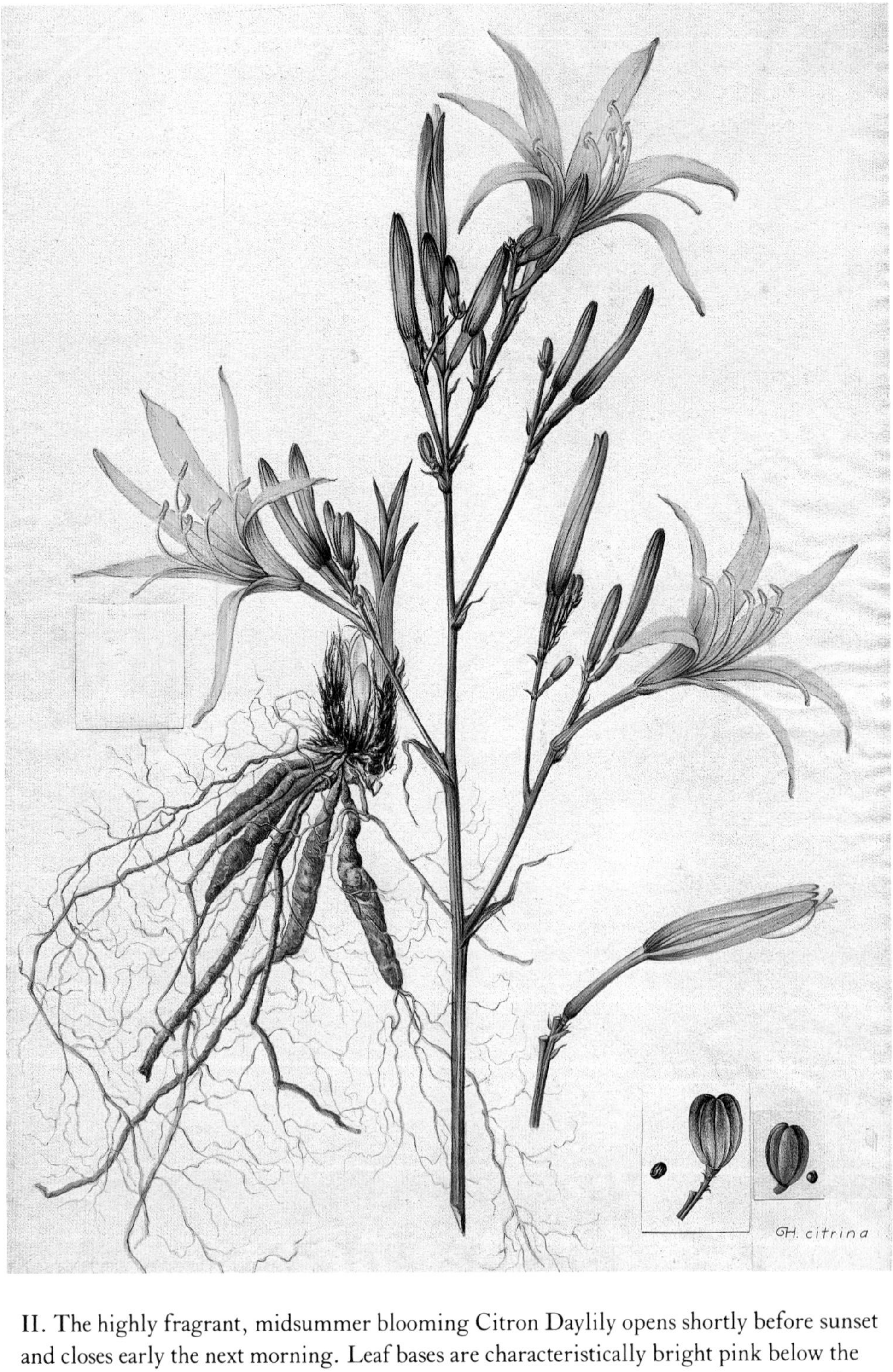

II. The highly fragrant, midsummer blooming Citron Daylily opens shortly before sunset and closes early the next morning. Leaf bases are characteristically bright pink below the soil line. The narrow-petaled flowers are borne on forty-five inch scapes. *Courtesy of The New York Botanical Garden Library.*

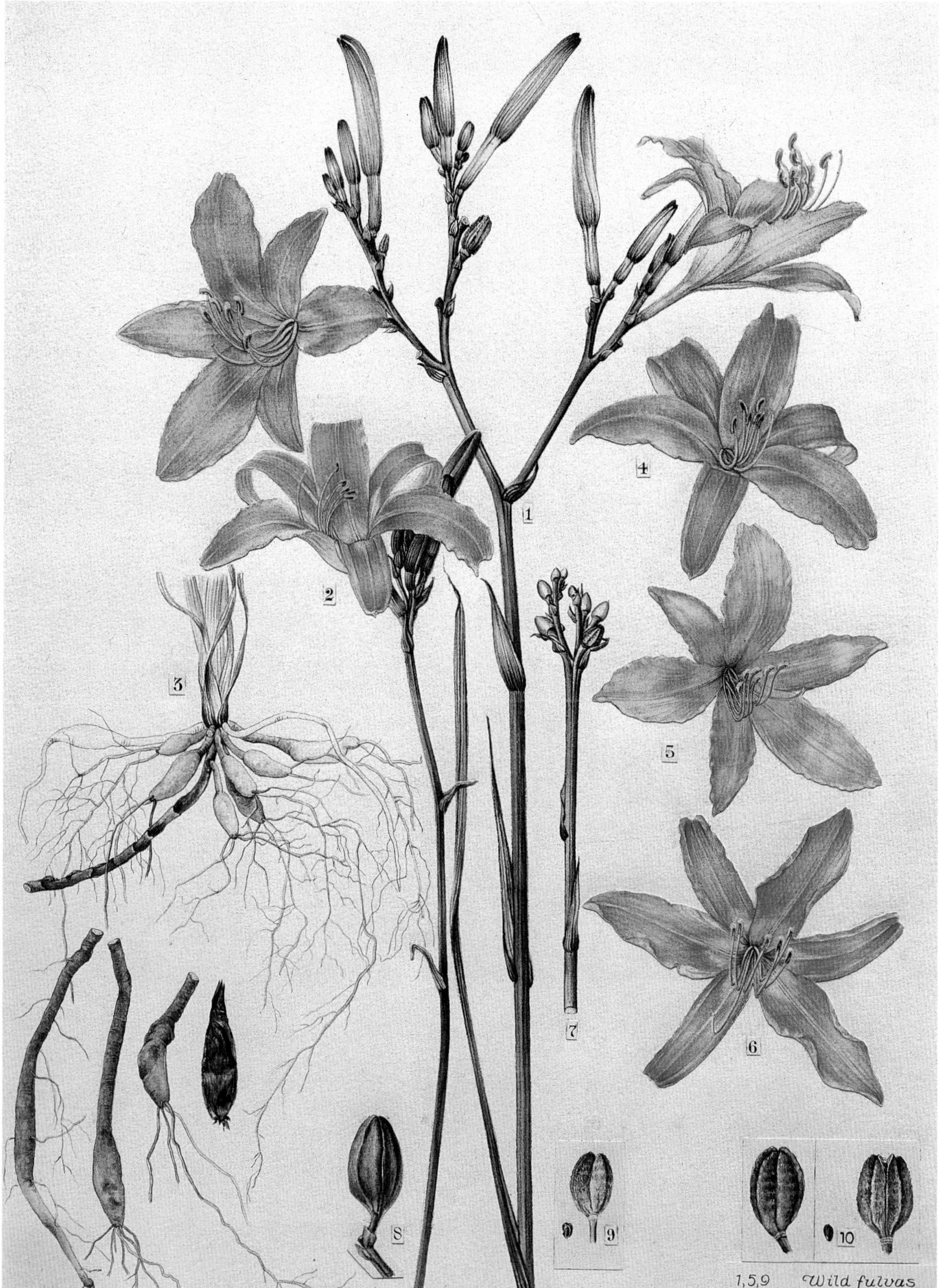

III. This study compares three fulvous daylilies. When compared to *Hemerocallis fulva*, *H. aurantiaca* has flower scapes that are shorter; leaves darker green and more evergreen; flowers less fulvous, lacking reticulation and opening less widely with narrower petals. Flowers of *H. littorea* are similar to *H. aurantiaca*, but with capsules more similar to *H. fulva*. *Courtesy of The New York Botanical Garden Library.*

IV. This plate illustrates daylily cultivars produced from various complex hybridizations of species hybrids. Colors range from the yellows and oranges of the species to the new shades of pink and red. *Courtesy of The New York Botanical Garden Library.*

DAYLILIES

The Wild Species and Garden Clones, Both Old and New, of the Genus Hemerocallis

A.B. Stout

Introduction and Updating by
Darrel Apps

Foreword by
Graham Stuart Thomas

A Ngaere Macray Book

Sagapress, Inc.
Sagaponack, New York

Copyright © 1986 by Sagapress, Inc.; a Ngaere Macray Book
All rights reserved

Library of Congress Cataloging-in-Publication Data:
Stout, Arlow Burdette, 1876–1957.
Daylilies: the wild species and garden clones,
both old and new, of the genus Hemerocallis.

"A Ngaere Macray book"
Reprint. Originally published: New York: Macmillan, 1934.
Bibliography: p. 111
Includes index.
1. Daylilies. I. Title.
SB413.D3S76 1986 635.9'34324 86-6477
ISBN 0-89831-028-8

Edited by Lois Fern
Designed by Joe Marc Freedman
Production Coordinated by Doreen Ralph

Distributed by
Timber Press, Inc.
9999 S.W. Wilshire, Suite 124
Portland, Oregon 97225

Printed in Hong Kong

Second Printing 1992

CONTENTS

APPENDIX

ILLUSTRATIONS

The colorplates in this 1986 edition are reproduced from original watercolors at the New York Botanical Garden Library. The artists were Eleanor Clarke and Mary Eaton. The plates were commissioned by A. B. Stout for a "Folio of the Genus Hemerocallis" [see Appendix B, no. 58] and paid for by a W.P.A. grant. The folio was never published due to lack of funding during the depression.

COLORPLATES

BLACK-AND-WHITE PLATES

INTRODUCTION TO THE 1986 EDITION

In the history and development of almost every organization there is one identifiable individual who has played a pivotal role in its success. Arlow Burdette Stout (1876-1957) was that person for the American Hemerocallis Society. His book *Daylilies*, originally published in 1934 and reprinted here, is a testimonial to his contributions to scientific investigation and a treatise useful in understanding the subsequent development of new daylily flower colors and forms.

Sooner or later all *Hemerocallis* enthusiasts ask the question, "What were the original species like?" If they do their library research well, they find the answer in *Daylilies*. Familiarity with this ageless reference work has become the daylily breeder's symbol for "rite of passage," for not understanding its content means leaving out a valuable part of the past. How can you know where you are going unless you know where you have been?

It was the species and cultivar descriptions in this book that became the impetus for the first breeders in their development of modern daylilies. *Daylilies* enticed amateur gardeners to try their hands at hybridizing. In essence, it was the fuel that fired continuous generations of new daylily cultivars. It was this book that allowed members of the American Hemerocallis Society to move their plant ahead so fast that the general gardening public could not keep up!

Daylily enthusiasts have often lamented the fact that the infinite potential of their favorite flower has been undiscovered by many gardeners. But in the last decade, a resurgence of perennial gardening in the United States has inspired even nonzealots, and now gardeners everywhere are beginning to talk about daylilies. Last year they were the top sales item for Wayside Gardens and White Flower Farm, prompting leading mail-order business executives to ponder over the possibility of exhausting their daylily inventories. Indeed, a sort of daylily mania is here and seems to be spreading from gardener to gardener and country to country.

Although the bulk of the breeders is found in the United States, breeder groups have started in Great Britain, Australia, New Zealand, Germany, and Japan. Newly expressed interest extends from exporters in the Netherlands to garden collectors in the republics of Korea and China. Because of recent advances made by breeders in southern Florida, even the tropics are potential sites.

Today most professional horticulturists recognize the potential of daylilies. For the most part, they are carefree plants filling temperate-zone landscapes with bright colors during the hottest, most difficult part of the garden year. But the real excitement in growing them is the daily landscape change, for individual blossoms last only a day, even though flower stalks may have blooms for up to six weeks. Each dawn offers the gardener the thrill of a fresh palette and a new painting. With judicious cultivar selection, the crescendos can go on all summer.

Few but the ingenious Arlow Burdette Stout would have envisioned the latent sources of beauty hidden in the raw materials of yellow and orange species daylilies. Although an Englishman, George Yeld, is the first person known to have bred species daylilies, Dr. Stout was the first to gather diploid breeding forms of fulvous daylilies and the first to breed extensively with *Hemerocallis fulva rosea*. When these were crossed with light yellow species and cultivars, they produced seedlings in a wide range of colors, from light pink to deep red.

Although Americans are often known for their ingenuity, the story of the development of the modern daylily in America encompasses some incredible good luck. Early America had not one single daylily species. Like the new settlers, the first daylilies to arrive — the Lemon Daylily, *Hemerocallis lilio-asphodelus* (*H. flava*), and the Tawny Daylily, *Hemerocallis fulva* 'Europa' —

were immigrants. Unlike the people though, the two daylilies did not intermarry and have children. For one reason, they bloomed at different times; for another, the Tawny Daylily was pod sterile. However, it did propagate sexually by rhizomatous new shoots. In fact, its weedy nature greatly disturbed early farmers who found they couldn't kill it! Nonetheless, when the pioneers moved westward, wives often concealed with their other valued possessions a few Tawny Daylilies to add cheer to what was often a cheerless new environment.

As the daylily continued to be a favorite among the settlers, its next stroke of luck occurred when Arlow Stout's mother planted a Tawny Daylily next to the porch of their Albion, Wisconsin, home. (There are those who might argue that rather than luck it was the ageless good sense or premonition of a woman.) Regardless, this plant and its family relative *Lilium tigrinum*, at the other end of the porch, produced no seed pods; and this caused young "Bert" to wonder why.

In actuality, Stout's inquisition as to why seed pods didn't form spans some thirty-seven years — from the time he was sixteen until he was fifty-three. His academic training, career choice, and research unfold like a predetermined plan to answer this question. Finally, in 1929, in a collaborative cytological work with Torasabura Susa, Dr. Stout published the answer in *Annals of the New York Academy of Sciences* (31: 1-30). He had discovered that the Tawny Daylily is a triploid and is usually sterile because of irregular sporogenesis. Since it is nonbreeding and has to be propagated asexually, he assigned the cultivar designation 'Europa'. That is not to say that he didn't have some success breeding the Tawny Daylily. The 4 December 1926 *Florist Exchange* reports that he made 7,135 cross-pollinations. From these crosses he got twenty-three mature *Hemerocallis fulva* 'Europa' seed capsules containing seventy seeds. Eleven seedlings were eventually raised, all from a wild Chinese *H. fulva* pollen parent. He also got over twelve hundred seedlings by using *H. fulva* 'Europa' as a pollen parent with other daylily plants.

Not surprisingly, Dr. Stout mentioned the sterile Tawny Daylily next to the porch of his boyhood home in his autobiography. The modest plant had ignited the first sparks of an illustrious career.

The byproducts of Arlow Burdette Stout's cytological work — species and cultivar collection, taxonomic keys, hybridization, and cultivar description — led to a publication that ultimately played a vital role in the formation of the American Hemerocallis Society. The book, *Daylilies*, offered a wealth of practical information on species and new cultivars and established Dr. Stout as a daylily authority. Further work from 1935 to 1941 in *Herbertia*, a publication of the American Plant Life Society, kept the Stout name before the gardening public. By 1946, with World War II over, gardening enthusiasm was enjoying an international revival. Midwestern American gardeners encouraged Iowa's Henry Field Seed Company to resume its popular prewar flower shows. Marie Anderson, coordinator of the "Round Robin Reserves" (a chain letter), suggested that the new flower show feature the "in-vogue" plant, the daylily. Shenandoah, Iowa, radio announcer Helen Field Fischer agreed to cover the show, and the promotion was on. On 13 July 1946, the public came to the show, and the "Garden Club of the Air" entertained. The crowd was much larger than expected and many stayed over. The next day, the Midwest Hemerocallis Society was formed, and by the end of the charter year, 757 members had paid the $3.00 dues. At its 1947 convention, the society had forty-three states, England, and Canada represented. A name change that year brought forth the American Hemerocallis Society, and to this day, Arlow Burdette Stout is credited with key contributions to the formation of the present 3672-member society.

Arlow Stout died in 1957 at the age of eighty-one. He left a legacy of over 350 scientific papers. Few daylily enthusiasts realize the breadth of his scientific investigations beyond those that relate to their favorite plant.

In the academic year 1921-22, while a visiting member of the faculty of Pomona College in southern California, Dr. Stout developed a special interest concerning irregularities in the fruiting and nonfruiting of avocados. He found that the pollen from the stamens of flowers on one tree fertilized pistils of the flowers on another tree only in the forenoon, while pistils of the flower on the first tree accepted pollen from stamens on the flowers of another tree only in the afternoon. This research revolutionized the avocado industry, and subsequently modified planting systems are still used today.

In cooperation with the New York State Agricultural Experiment Station, Arlow Stout produced 175 new seedless-grape varieties of the Mediterranian type hardy in northern areas. Dr. H. A. Gleason, head curator at the New York Botanical Garden, told its board of managers at their 1936 annual meeting: "It is not unlikely that the commercial value of the work of Dr. Stout, director of the garden laboratory, will exceed the entire cost of the garden during the forty years of its history." The popular seedless-grape cultivar 'Himrod' was bred by Dr. Stout and introduced in 1942.

Dr. Stout studied sterility in potatoes over a period of several years with the United States Bureau of Plant Industry. In conjunction with this work, during the summers of 1921 through 1924, he researched pollen viability on several clonal potato varieties at Presque Isle, Maine.

From 1924 until 1931, he directed extensive projects of hybridization of *Populus* species under the auspices of the Oxford Paper Company. This project was later continued with the Forest Service of the United States Department of Agriculture.

Arlow Stout's other investigative research — besides daylilies — included apples, cherries, chicory, Chinese Cabbage, coleus, date palms, lilies, lily-of-the-valley, lobelia, moss pink, narcissus, Norway Maple, peas, petunia, and sweet potatoes. These studies arose from his interests in genetics and the phenomenon of sterility in plants.

By his own rather elaborate accounting system, Dr. Stout recorded his publication of ninety-seven different daylily papers in popular magazines, scientific journals, and books. When Stout died in 1957, Farr Nursery of Womelsdorf, Pennsylvania, reported that it had introduced eighty-three clones of his daylilies and still had twelve double selections it was considering. 'Dauntless', one of his 1935 cultivar registrations, received the American Hemerocallis Society's highest award in 1954 — the coveted Stout Medal, named in his honor.

Financing of the Stout Medal — first awarded in 1950 — had been derived from royalties Stout declined from the Farr Nursery Company. Daylilies had been removed from the New York Botanical Garden in 1934 because of an edict from the director, Dr. N. L. Britton. (Britton had decided that "the garden could not propagate daylilies either for general distribution or for sale.") When no nursery from the New York area was interested in handling these plants, a letter to businesses in outlying areas elicited a single response — from nurseryman Bertrand H. Farr.

One might presume that Dr. Stout's vocational and avocational interests were totally within the plant-science areas. This was, indeed, his focus in the later years of his life. However, as a young man growing up in Wisconsin, his interests expanded well beyond plants. Three-fourths of the area around Albion, Wisconsin, was uncultivated in the 1880s and it was in this untouched wilderness that Arlow and his brother, Claude, learned about "the land."

Lake Koshkonong, a large shallow lake near their home, was a mecca for both aquatic and forest birds. Arlow studied them intently. He had a blacksmith make him a pair of climbing irons and with them he climbed the tallest trees, peering into birds' nests. On one occasion he discovered two red-tailed-hawk's eggs — but in their recovery fell and badly bruised himself! These eggs remained prized possessions throughout his life.

It was also in this environment that Stout met Ludwig Kumlein, son of the famous Thure Kumlein, an internationally known naturalist who mounted birds for the public museum of Milwaukee, the University of Wisconsin, and the Smithsonian Institution. From him, Arlow learned of physical geography, ornithology, and natural history. He purchased an 1893 taxidermy book by William T. Horniday and became expert in mounting specimens.

From very early life Arlow Stout had an interest in books. A favorite was Elliot Coues's *Key to North American Birds* (1894). He paid $7.50 for it in the 1890s, earning the money by selling raw furs of minks, muskrats, and skunks that he had trapped. Two books that he purchased in college remained in his working collection throughout his career: *Laboratory of Botany* by C. H. Clark and *Elementary Botany* by G. F. Atkinson, both 1898 editions.

While teaching near Baraboo, Wisconsin, Dr. Stout published in the *Wisconsin Archeologist* (1906), a descriptive survey of the archeology of eastern Sauk County. In the area is a remarkable 214-foot-long Indian effigy mound. Realizing its fragile position, Stout helped to raise the money necessary for purchasing and preserving the land holding this treasure.

In collaboration with a friend, H. L. Skavlem, Stout surveyed all of the Indian mounds around Lake Koshkonong before they were destroyed by cultivation. The report of this survey was also published in the *Wisconsin Archeologist* (1908).

In the summers of 1908 and 1909, A. B. Stout was employed by the North Dakota Historical Society in making surveys of the Mandan, Aribara, and Hidatsa Indians. Of special interest were the turtle effigies that the Mandan Indians had carefully laid out on the prairies of the state. Stout mapped, numbered, and bagged every stone of one, which he then had transported and reconstructed on the grounds of the state capitol at Bismarck.

A. B. Stout's former associates at the New York Botanical Garden replied in various ways to a question about what he was like, but all replied in the same vein: "...straight-laced, highly reserved, and no nonsense." "He was very direct." "...no great sense of humor." "...out at 6:00 A.M." "...positive man with courage of conviction." "...impatient with fools." These responses reflect a serious quality which is understandable, considering the difficult economic times of his childhood and early adult years. Arlow Stout himself describes a memorable incident from those lean times: "I was a teacher in a modest little country school house with an attendance of 35 pupils....I saved $300.00 which were on deposit in a bank and I planned to enter the State Normal at Whitewater, Wisconsin, in the autumn of 1898. But before that time arrived the bank failed due to the defalcation of the cashier who fled to Canada and there lived in immunity. Ultimately I obtained about $30.00 of my savings."

Dr. Stout was born in Ohio in 1876 and moved as an infant to

Albion, Wisconsin, reportedly because of his parents' interest in the famous Albion Academy established by "ship captains and college graduates." He attended public schools and subsequently had one winter term of study at Milton College and two terms at Albion Academy. He taught in rural schools for three years. In 1903 he graduated from the State Normal School at Whitewater, Wisconsin. Then, for four years (1903–7) he was a high-school science teacher in Baraboo, Wisconsin. In 1907 he began studies at the University of Wisconsin, majoring in botany under the directorship of R. A. Harper. His bachelor of arts degree was awarded in June 1909 (he attained both Phi Beta Kappa and Sigma Xi). During 1908 and 1909 he was an assistant in Botany, then an instructor from 1909 to 1911. He married Zelda Judd Howe in 1909 and had one daughter. In 1911 he joined the scientific staff of the New York Botanical Garden. Stout earned his Ph.D. from Columbia University in February 1913.

During his career at the New York Botanical Garden from 1911 to 1948, as Director of Laboratories first, and later as Curator of Education and Laboratories, Stout received many awards. Among them were the Thomas Howland Medal of the Massachusetts Horticultural Society, the gold medal of the Horticulture Society of New York, the William Herbert Medal of the American Amaryllis Society, the Bertrand Farr Award for Hemerocallis Improvement, and a Distinguished Service Award from the New York Botanical Garden. He was also granted honorary life memberships in the Royal Horticultural Society, the Horticulture Society of New York, and the Pennsylvania Horticultural Society.

With daylily interest at an all-time high and gardeners hungry for plant literature, it seems only appropriate that the work of this renowned scientist be reprinted. Serious amateur gardeners have much to learn from its text and from its many black-and-white illustrations and beautiful colorplates of species and cultivars. Individuals interested in heirloom plants can at last find some descriptive information; societies, such as Great Britain's National Council for the Conservation of Plants and Gardens, can use this book as an important reference; students will find use for species descriptions and taxonomic keys, since little progress has been made beyond the information presented.

Now, finally, all those members of daylily clubs, and other enthusiasts, who for years have hoped this book would one day be reprinted, will have a chance to add it to their garden reference collections. And the hierarchy of the American Hemerocallis Society can once again demand its use for "rite of passage!"

Darrel Apps, Ph.D.

Dr. Darrel Apps heads the Department of Education at Longwood Gardens, Kennett Square, Pennsylvania. He is a long-time member of the American Hemerocallis Society having served as regional vice-president from 1980 to 1981 and scientific editor from 1982 to 1984. He has published articles on daylilies in the Daylily Journal, *the* Proceedings of the International Plant Propagation Society, *and the* Canadian Journal of Botany. *In 1984 he spent six weeks on a U.S. Department of Agriculture plant-collection trip to remote Korean islands collecting daylily species. Dr. Apps is an active daylily hybridizer who has registered twenty cultivars. His hybrid 'Pardon Me' won the 1985 Donn Fischer Award for the best miniature daylily.*

FOREWORD TO THE 1986 EDITION

It is not growing like a tree
In bulk, doth make Man better be;
Or standing long an oak, three hundred year,
To fall a log at last, dry, bald, and sere:
A lily of a day
Is fairer far in May,
Although it fall and die that night —
It was the plant and flower of Light.
In small proportions we just beauties see;
And in short measures life may perfect be.

Ben Jonson,
1573 – 1637

We do not know at what age Jonson wrote the above lines. He lived for sixty-four years, dying in 1637; the thoughts put into the poem perhaps indicate that he was of mature years. He survived his children, which is apposite both to his poem and to us. Among his more famous compositions is the song "Drink to me only with thine eyes," but he was popular at the court of James I for his masques and plays. His life span was closely echoed by that of Inigo Jones, famous as an architect of churches, houses, and bridges. Who shall say that the magnificence of a stone or brick edifice — slowly, slowly decaying — can equal the beauty of a flower, fresh every day, or the immortality of words? *Hemerocallis* means the "beauty of a day" — the plant or flower of light: Jonson's poem is a "flower of light" too.

It was during Jonson's span of years that the Pilgrim Fathers landed at Massachusetts in 1620, and nine years later John Parkinson wrote his great book *Paradisi in sole paradisus terrestris*, one of the first books to extol the beauty of flowers, as opposed to their usefulness. *Hemerocallis flava* and *H. fulva* were in cultivation in England at that time. It was, indeed, the beginning of worldwide travel and the bringing to Europe, through the efforts of the Portuguese, Spanish, French, Dutch, and English, of many new plants. Parkinson was enthralled with the great flowers of tulip and iris, rose and lily — in fact many of the largest and most splendid flowers find a place in the earliest pages of this work. It was perhaps fortunate that so many flamboyant flowers had bulbous roots — which made transport comparatively easy — and that many of these same bulbous plants were natives of the countries around the Mediterranean.

Centuries ago, many plants from the Far East were brought to Europe through commerce, over land or by sea. Chinese dominions at one time extended as far as the Caspian Sea, facilitating land transport, but alternatively, like perhaps the Crimson China rose, the daylily may have entered Europe through French agency in Madagascar. One thing is certain, that, with the iris and the rose, any plant with a lily-like flower was greatly treasured in Europe for its beauty, apart from its use as a food — and in China, the bulbs of several lilies were cooked as food and the flowers of the daylily were used medicinally and as a delicacy to add to a dish.

There is no doubt that from the dawn of civilization, in the Far East and in the West, flowers have been sought and treasured, at first for their practical value — imaginary or real — but later for their beauty. It seems to me that those of us who continue to search for the beauty of flowers bestow a blessing not only on ourselves but on others by influence. We have so ransacked the world for flowers that in the more temperate climates of north and south there is not a week of the year passes — except when frost holds all in its iron grip — when there is nothing in flower. Every year the pageantry of flowers starts with the snowdrop and aconite; before they are finished the earliest daffodils and hyacinths appear, to be quickly followed by the tulips and irises. As the air warms so the scene becomes even more enriched, working up to the magnificence of peonies, roses, and lilies.

We never tire of the progression. The flowers greet us afresh in their season yearly. I do not want chrysanthemums and roses in my garden throughout the year any more than bananas and oranges constantly on my table. Each flower exerts a spell upon us, each has its season, and the season of each is elongated by early and late varieties. Yet I have noted, over the years, that while lovers of flowers are always entranced by an early form of a favorite, late kinds are not so welcomed. We are then moving on to the next display in the pageant.

But what have we in daylilies? *Hemerocallis flava*, the Lemon Daylily, is not only the first to flower but it is also the first lily of any size to produce its blooms, which open in early June in England. We are then poised in anticipation of the opening of the lily season, and there is no doubt that this gracious, easily grown plant has considerable influence upon us. Moreover this lily is easy of culture and it produces a dense group of graceful leaves which remain in fresh green until their demise in a brief flash of yellow in autumn. The flowers are borne for about three or four weeks and have a pronounced and delicious fragrance. Through hybridization, daylilies now come upon us in a great variety of colors and sizes. These variations are not *created* by the ardent hybridists; rather do they select seedlings which please them, knowing full well that all colors are inherent in the different species and only await cross-pollination in order to be released. It is as well, when contemplating a great range of seedlings, to decide in advance what are the criteria that make a good daylily. Not size alone, nor color, but a fusion of these with a true lily-shaped flower — an open trumpet — borne well aloft above the foliage, which should be beautifully arched and not coarse or twisted. For garden value we should select self-colors, because however exquisite at close quarters those with a pattern of diverse colorings may be, their interest and value are lost at a distance. We favor a compact, not a stoloniferous root, unless it is required for extensive naturalising, in which case a parentage involving *H. fulva* will be preferred. The stems, besides bearing the flowers well above the foliage, should be reasonably erect and not splay outwards beyond the foliage. And we want fragrance as well if we can get it.

Apart from saying that the light colors are most telling in the garden landscape I should not presume to dictate the choice. But it is interesting that the vast range of peach, pink, red, maroon, and mauve colorings derive from only one species, *H. fulva* and its variety *rosea*. All the others are of some tone of yellow or orange. As the eye sweeps round the garden, it is these yellows and also the orange, apricot, and pale peach tints that are at once picked out. The more subtle, even subdued tones are much sought today; they are the fanciers' pieces. Coupled with frilled or gophered segments, perhaps with the segments reflexed into almost a ball and the original trumpet shape lost, they are best appreciated on the table beside one, or on the show bench. Who can dispute that they are triumphs of the selectors, the colors put forth by nature? And while on this sort of subject we should remember a few doubles; though doubling adds nothing to the beauty of a lily of any sort, double flowers normally last longer than singles, with a correspondingly greater garden value.

Many years ago a white variety was selected by the famous nurseryman Amos Perry at Enfield, north of London. It was subsequently lost, but we hear of new whites, and near-whites, from the United States. We can surmise that white would come mainly from the influence of *H. fulva*. It would be the result of a sudden "sport" to white rather than a development from the pale yellow species such as *H. citrina* and *H. flava*. It is a strange fact that white sports crop up in nature and in cultivation much more frequently from flowers of tints between the red and the blue of the spectrum than among yellows. We should welcome a true white with open arms, although it would be far removed from that most exquisite of all lilies, the Madonna, or *Lilium candidum*.

The danger is that with too much selection in one direction we open the door to disease in any genus, and it is important to bring in as many species as possible from time to time. Not only is this a help in combating disease, but it saves the strain being of plants of one height and therefore of one sort of use in gardens. There is such potential in the genus *Hemerocallis*. We know now that dwarf species can give us a range of coloring in plants under a foot in height. Others can exceed four feet in height. Whatever their height, their season, their style or color, they will generously fit in with all sorts of planting, formal and informal, in beds and borders or naturally grouped in thin woodland. (I think there is even a future for night-blooming kinds, to be derived from *H. citrina* so long as its coarse dull foliage can be bred out. Flowering as most do when the nights are warm, they would be of special use to decorate the floodlit gardens of restaurants which keep open until a late hour.) In placing any daylilies in the garden where attention is paid to individual heights, it is important to remember that it is the height of the clump of foliage that dictates the position. The flowers, perhaps borne well aloft, last only for three or four weeks.

In July and August, when most of the species and the hybrids flower, there are at hand two genera liking the same conditions which complement daylilies supremely well in color and habit — phloxes, and the hardy lobelias (which are crosses between *Lobelia cardinalis*, *L. fulgens*, *and L. syphylitica*). Superb contrasts and blends of colors can be worked out. In more shady places we have yet another genus of great worth and contrast in color and shape of foliage —*Hosta*.

If early species like *H. flava* are brought into the strain freely, the bearded irises will hardly be over before we shall have the daylilies upon us. And here I will sound another note of warning. I feel it to be undesirable to proceed along stereotyped lines in breeding not only on account of disease but because it allows breeders to conjure up ever more complex shapes and patterns. It has happened already with the irises which have now lost their classic shape in a welter of frills and flounces. Daylily cultivars are also, some of them, being selected with too much attention to outlandish shapes and frills. Let us not forget the classic lily shape. *H. fulva* 'Maculata' sets a poise, a shape, and a vigor that is hard to beat.

I like to think that these evolutions from a primordial ancestor are not just due to general evolution from plants of a much more primitive nature through a chance combination of gases and chemicals, as scientists would have us believe. If all is due to chance, whence came the daylily's desire to please the insects that have pollinated it for untold millions of years? And how came they to know that they would please a much later arrival on this planet, man?

It is extraordinary that daylilies, which have been known to Western civilization for so many centuries and which are such reliable garden plants, remained in obscurity for so long. As recently as a hundred years ago, only the few principal species were grown and no hybrids were recorded. However, one enthusiast, George Yeld, saw possibilities for hybridization and improvement from a garden point of view. He was born in 1843 and lived for ninety-five years. In early life he was a master at St. Peter's School, York, and after retirement he lived near Gerrards Cross in Buckinghamshire. No doubt his interest in plants was fostered by visits to the nursery of James Backhouse of York which at the turn of the century carried an immense and varied stock of plants.

Yeld's first hybrid daylily was 'Apricot', named in 1892; he subsequently raised many others among which I remember 'Sirius', 'Radiant', and 'J. S. Gayner' being well known in the 1930s. The last named is still grown and has a very shapely flower of clear coloring; the others are seldom seen. (Yeld concerned himself not only with daylilies. In that same decade, some of his most noted bearded irises, such as 'Lord of June' and 'Asia', were in most gardens where irises were grown. Many are still seen today.)

The interest started by Yeld was soon taken up by Amos Perry, whose father (of the same name) had started a nursery at Winchmore Hill in north London. The second Amos died in 1953 leaving a vast number of plants of his raising, most of which have disappeared. He raised and named over a hundred varieties of daylily, some of the more famous and lasting being 'Thelma Perry', 'Margaret Perry', and 'George Yeld'. Such was the prolificity of output of hybrid plants from Enfield and so enticing were Amos Perry's catalogues, that W. E. Gumbleton, a witty Irish gardener and keen plantsman, described him as "the minor Prophet of Enfield."

In Naples, Italy, the firm of Wilhelm Müller also contributed to the stream. After the Second World War, raisers to the fore in

England were H. J. Randall, L. W. Brummitt, Norton Hall Nurseries, and Lady Carew Pole. But this line of breeders seems to have died out in England; nobody today is busy raising hybrids, and nurserymen give little attention to these splendid garden plants. On the Continent, and especially in Germany and the Netherlands, the story is different and most herbaceous nurseries list a good number. Enthusiasm is also waxing in the Southern Hemisphere and in Japan. Many raisers of today find their seedlings benefit from the exchange of pollen from advanced hybrids from the United States.

Preceding the brief history of daylily development immediately above, I indicated a few of the assets of daylilies. Most gardeners have in their mind's eye a vague picture of them. Of varied colors, they are thought of as bold, grassy-leafed plants with wide open lily-flowers borne from three to four feet above ground. But this gives just the popular and most general conception. Daylilies have much else to offer.

At daffodil time, *Hemerocallis fulva* clones grow fast and early and show their pale green foliage to advantage, as a contrast to the rich green, broad leaves of colchicums and the general, rather grayish green of daffodils. Apart from our desire for flowers in the early year, I think we are all avid for new greenery to refresh us after the winter, during which the beautiful evergreens become progressively tawdry. *H. flava*, the Lemon Daylily, is usually the first in flower; not only is it an exquisite flower but it is perhaps the best scented of all (scent being a characteristic found also in many hybrids descended in part from it or related species of like coloring). Then follow the second earlies, such as the deep yellow *H. middendorfii* and *H. dumortieri*. The latter has brown on the outside of the outer segments, a tint traced also in 'Corky' and 'Golden Chimes'. While we all usually strive for larger and larger flowers, the small flowers of these kinds are a delightful contrast, and they are also found in *H. multiflora* whose flowers do not open until late in the season. *H. multiflora* is followed by the latest species of all, *H. exaltata*; this has unfortunately coarse leaves and rather inelegant clusters of flowers at the tops of tall stems. Meanwhile two dwarf species achieving barely a foot in height, *H. nana* and *H. minor*, have flowered, and *H. fulva* has also come into bloom.

So in England we have a long season of flowering, from early June to late August, and a big range of heights to choose from. Colors vary from light yellow (*H. citrina* and *H. flava*) through orange-yellow (from many species) to those of the supreme color-givers, the *H. fulva* clan. From the soft terracotta of the most common clone over here, that known as *H. fulva* 'Europa', to the magnificent 'Maculata' and variety *rosea* (unique in its soft pinkish coloring) there is a considerable range of tints. Due to the impact of the *fulva* clan, and particularly var. *rosea*, hybridists have today been able to give us all the colors in the spectrum save blue and its immediate tints. Even green and white are within grasp. Before and long after flowering, the clumps of arching leaves are good to look upon if their spent flowering stems be removed. Added to all these assets, many hybrids have fragrance, and all are tough, hardy garden plants thriving almost anywhere if their few needs are provided: they love sun but will put up with partial shade (or even full shade if it be from a high wall and not dense trees) and they require a well-nurtured soil. The only failure I have had with daylilies in England was in a cold, rather wet border in Northumberland.

Very few perennial plants have so many advantages for the gardener, and I hope that the republication of Dr. Stout's valuable book will bring home this fact to all.

Graham Stuart Thomas, OBE, VMH, DHM, VMM

Graham Stuart Thomas is Britain's foremost gardener and plantsman. He has been gardens consultant to the National Trust for many years and is the author of Gardens of the National Trust, Perennial Garden Plants, The Art of Planting, Climbing Roses Old and New, The Old Shrub Roses, Shrub Roses of Today, Plants for Ground Cover, Color in the Winter Garden, Three Gardens, *and* Trees in the Landscape.

Arlow Burdette Stout at his desk

PREFACE

It is the aim to present in this volume the most important information of interest and concern to gardeners and botanists regarding the species and the horticultural clones of the genus *Hemerocallis*. Attention is given to the synopsis and the description of the species, to the enumeration, description, and evaluation of the clonal varieties and to matters pertaining to the uses and the culture of these plants.

Much of the information is based on personal study and observation of living plants of which a rather complete collection has been assembled at The New York Botanical Garden. This collection includes (1) representatives of the know species, and, for several of these, plants have been obtained from the wild in various localities in Japan, China, Manchuria, and Siberia, (2) more than one hundred of the horticultural clones, and (3) several thousand seedlings produced by hybridization and selective breeding. Data have also been obtained and assembled from botanical and horticultural literature, from the catalogs and typed lists issued by nurserymen, from a rather extensive correspondence, and from personal consultation with various persons, including Mr. George Yeld and Mr. Amos Perry in England and Mr. Willy Müller in Italy.

The collection of daylilies available to the author for study at The New York Botanical Garden has been made possible largely through the generous contributions of nurserymen and growers and by the coöperation of those who have sent living plants and seeds of wild types from Japan, China, and Manchuria. A list of those concerned in these contributions has recently been published in the *Journal of The New York Botanical Garden* (**35**: 138–139. June 1933). Numerous individuals and nursery firms are mentioned in the text of this volume, and in the Appendix names and addresses are given and information is presented in respect to persons and institutions that have been most active in the development of daylilies or in their distribution or display. To all those thus noted and to all others not mentioned who have contributed directly or indirectly to this volume the writer wishes to express appreciation.

Certain portions of this volume have been presented, in substance at least, in various popular and semi-popular articles written by the author that have appeared in *House and Garden*, *Arts and Decoration*, *The Ladies Home Journal*, *New Silva and Flora*, and the *Journal of The New York Botanical Garden*. There have been also descriptions with colored plates of sixteen daylilies in *Addisonia* and also various articles of a more technical nature in botanical journals. Several of the illustrations in this volume are from the cuts used in articles published in the *Journal of The New York Botanical Garden* and the four colored plates are reproduced from *Addisonia*, and these are here used by permission. To the authorities of The New York Botanical Garden the writer is also greatly indebted for the facilities and support that have made possible those studies of which this volume is a product.

ARLOW BURDETTE STOUT

January, 1934.

DAYLILIES

THE WILD SPECIES AND GARDEN CLONES, BOTH OLD AND NEW, OF THE GENUS

HEMEROCALLIS

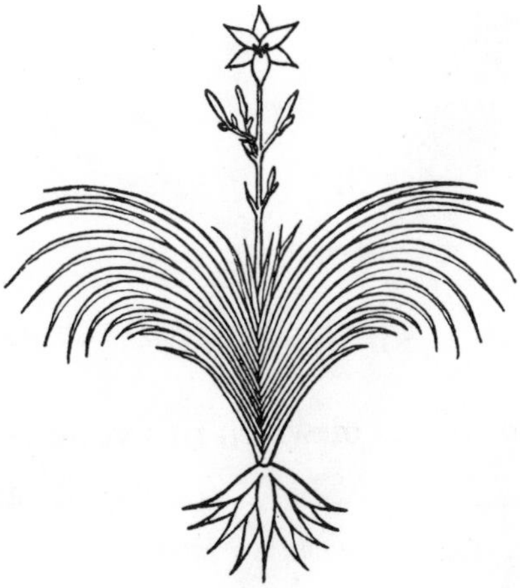

Plate 1. The Lemon Daylily (*Hemerocallis flava*)

CHAPTER I

THE BOTANICAL CHARACTERISTICS OF DAYLILIES

In appearance, habits of growth, and botanical characteristics, the daylilies form a rather sharply defined group of plants known as the genus *Hemerocallis* of the Lily Family.

The daylilies are all herbaceous perennials. The parts which appear above ground and are conspicuous as the plants grow in gardens are the leaves, the flower stalks or scapes, and the flowers. The stems are in the soil or extending slightly above its surface. In temperate regions the foliage of most daylilies dies to the ground in autumn or is killed during early winter and the plant is dormant until spring arrives. In the tropics many daylilies are evergreen.

The leaves of daylilies are linear, strongly ribbed, and arranged in two ranks that are closely compacted and equitant at the base and that spread gracefully above to form a symmetrical "fan." In the disposition, height, and color of the leaves there is considerable diversity among species and garden clones.

The flower stalks or scapes arise directly from the crown in the midst of a cluster of leaves. They are naked except for leaf-like bracts at the few nodes and subtending the branches and the flowers. The scapes are slender, erect or ascending, and branched or unbranched at the top according to the character of the species.

The flowers of daylilies are large and colorful. In the general appearance of the perianth, six stamens, and single pistil they resemble the flowers of the genus *Lilium;* but they are shorter lived, in some types lasting for one day only, and the six segments of the showy perianth are united at the base to form a well-defined tube. The flower colors for the different species range from pale yellow through shades of yellow and orange to combinations with fulvous red. In the newer hybrids the colors have been extended especially into rosy pink, red, and purplish shades.

The fruit of daylilies is a dry dehiscent capsule of three chambers with numerous black rounded or somewhat angled seeds.

The stems of a daylily form a compact group or crown of numerous more or less interwoven branches with the leaf and flower-stalk buds at or near the surface of the soil. For some types, as the *Hemerocallis Dumortierii* (plate 36), all the crown-branches are short, erect, and much compacted. In types with more spreading habits of growth, as the various members of the species *H. fulva* (plate 35), rhizomes extend laterally in the soil sometimes to a distance of a foot or more. A rather vigorous natural propagation by the extension of the underground branches is a characteristic of the daylilies.

The roots of daylilies are numerous, divided into many fibrous branches, and rather deeply penetrating in the soil. In certain species, as the *Hemerocallis Middendorffii,* the main roots are merely slender-cylindrical; in others, as the *H. Thunbergii,* the mid-section of some of the main roots may be very slightly enlarged; in several species (especially *H. Dumortierii, H. flava, H. multiflora,* and *H. fulva*) many of the roots are noticeably swollen and enlarged, and in some cases the roots that are most fleshy end abruptly and have few fibrous branches.

For a time (Thunberg's *Flora Japonica.* 1784) the plantain lilies were included in the genus *Hemerocallis.* But these plants have only fibrous roots, mostly broad plantain-like leaves, flowers in simple unbranched racemes, flower colors in white, lilac, or blue, and winged seeds. It was soon realized by botanists that these plants should be considered as distinct from the daylilies.

The gardener will encounter no difficulties in recognizing the daylilies and in distinguishing them from the true lilies *(Lilium),* from the plantain lilies *(Hosta),* and from other important groups of garden plants of the Lily Family.

CHAPTER II

NAMES OF DAYLILIES

SOME of the daylilies grown in gardens are to be included with the natural or wild species and their varieties, but the greater number are plants that have been derived from the wild types by hybridization and selective breeding.

In nursery practice and in garden culture, all the daylilies are propagated by division. A plant is divided and thus multiplied until after successive divisions it exists as a large number of separate plants all of which are, however, merely branches of the one original seedling. Such a group of plants is known as a *clone,*[1] which is thus to be distinguished from a group of plants of a true *variety* each plant of which is a seedling.

When a cultivated clone of a daylily has been derived from a plant of a wild species or variety and is representative of that type, the proper botanical name for the species is often employed in speaking of the clone. Thus we have in garden culture plants of *Hemerocallis Thunbergii,* of *H. flava,* of *H. Dumortierii,* etc., and to these are also given common names such as Thunberg's Daylily, Lemon Daylily, and Dumortier's Daylily. But such a term is a general name for a group of plants and includes *all* the plants of the species.

As long as there is no marked variation in the clones of a species that may be in cultivation the specific name is sufficient for the gardener's needs. But the species of daylilies are variable and the differences between clones of a single species are often

[1] The term clon (klŏn or klōn), from the Greek *κλών* meaning a twig or slip, was suggested for this usage by Dr. Herbert J. Webber in 1903 (*Science* II. **18**: 501–503). Recently, various writers have used the spelling "clone" which more clearly requires the pronunciation "klōn."

sufficient to be of importance in horticulture. There are several somewhat different plants in culture under each of the names *H. flava*, *H. aurantiaca*, *H. Thunbergii*, and *H. Dumortierii* and the gardener is often puzzled by the differences. It is only by giving each of the different clones an individual or horticultural name that they can be designated properly and definitely identified in the trade and in garden culture.

The clonal name is merely a non-Latinized *special* name that is capitalized and which approaches in usage the rank of a proper noun. Fortunately, the large majority of the clones of daylilies which have been derived from hybrid seedlings have been given horticultural names, such as Apricot, Mikado, Margaret Perry, Tangerine, and Yellow Hammer. This nomenclature may be continued and extended to all clones that possess special or individual character.

In the earlier botanical and horticultural literature the emphasis was often placed on scientific or botanical names and certain clones were given Latinized names of specific or true varietal rank. Thus the old familiar *H. fulva* of Linnaeus is now recognized to be one of many very distinct clones of this species. Furthermore it is a triploid and it possesses a rather special combination of characters not duplicated in any other plant or clone. In order to distinguish definitely this clone, it has been proposed to call it *H. fulva* clone Europa or merely Europa Daylily. The same consideration may be given to the clones which were named as true varieties, such as *H. fulva* clone Maculata and *H. fulva* clone Cypriana.

Perhaps the most misleading names that have been employed for daylilies and other perennials propagated asexually are names of the rank of species that are given to clones that are developed from hybrid seedlings. A conspicuous case of this is the combination "*Hemerocallis luteola*," which was used for one or more seedlings of known hybrid origin. The attempt has been made to adopt the placing of an "×" after the generic name, as "*Hemerocallis* × *luteola*," to indicate hybrid origin. This is based on the idea, which is often incorrect, that the hybrids of two species are so nearly alike that they can be grouped together under one name. At least for horticultural plants propagated asexually, the identification of each clone is often necessary and this can best be indicated and preserved by such names as Luteola Daylily, Corona Daylily, and Florham Daylily.

Thus there are (I) **botanical** names, such as "*Hemerocallis multiflora*" the "Many flowered Daylily," which include all the members of a certain wild species of daylilies; and there are (II) **horticultural** names, (1) as "Bijou Daylily" for clones developed from individual seedlings of hybrid origin and (2) as "Europa Daylily" for individual clones of variable species.

CHAPTER III

THE NATURAL DISTRIBUTION OF DAYLILIES

Truly wild and indigenous daylilies evidently exist only in Asia, where they have a natural distribution over an extensive area of the central and northern parts of the continent including the more northerly of the islands to the east. They are reported from Siberia and Manchuria, as far south as Nepal and as far west as the Caucasus. It is sometimes stated that the types long in cultivation in European gardens are also indigenous in certain localities in Europe but it is most probable that the supposed wild daylilies of that region are escapes from cultivation, quite as the fulvous Europa Daylily has escaped and spread by vegetative propagation in many of the older settled areas of the United States.

The species of *Hemerocallis* now recognized are known in flower gardens and in botanical gardens in Europe and America from the relatively few individuals that have been brought into cultivation and propagated mostly as clones. Botanical collections and descriptions also contribute to the knowledge of the wild daylilies. Several species have been discovered rather recently. There are several groups of plants obtained from the Orient now growing at The New York Botanical Garden which do not conform to any of the species thus far described.

Without doubt there remain in the Orient other species and wild types yet to be discovered and brought into cultivation.

Plate 2. *Hemerocallis minor* and *H. flava*

Plate 3. Europa Daylily (*H. fulva* clone Europa)

Plate 4. *Hemerocallis nana*, in a six-inch pot

Plate 5. *Hemerocallis Thunbergii*

CHAPTER IV

DAYLILIES IN HISTORICAL RETROSPECT

Two daylilies had already found their way into the gardens of western Europe when the first books dealing with garden plants were printed. One of these, the Lemon Daylily of today (plates 1 and 2), was described by Pena and Lobel (*Historia*) in 1570 under the name *Asphodelus luteus liliflorus* as having yellow flowers, angular capsules, and black seeds. Six years later Lobel published a wood cut, which is the first illustration of a daylily, showing an entire plant of the Lemon Daylily with flowers and capsules, and with the fleshy roots and creeping rootstocks clearly indicating the habit of vegetative reproduction. At this time Lobel also described under the name *Liriosphodelus phoeniceus* a single-flowered daylily with cinnabar-red coloring in the flowers. This is the Europa Daylily of today (plate 3).

For nearly two hundred years following the record of Lobel, writers on garden plants mention these two daylilies under various names. Evidently they first received the generic name *Hemerocallis* when Linnaeus published his first edition of *Species Plantarum* in 1753. His name for the yellow-flowered one was *Hemerocallis Lilio-Asphodelus* var. *flavus*, and the fulvous one he called *Hemerocallis Lilio-Asphodelus* var. *fulvus*. At that time he considered the latter to be a hybrid, probably because its fruits and seeds were then unknown. Later, in the second edition of *Species Plantarum* (1762), he gave both plants specific rank under the names *H. flava* and *H. fulva*, and these botanical names have been universally accepted since that date. Linnaeus included with these two a plant which he called *Hemerocallis Liliastrum* but this plant is now placed in the genus *Paradisea*.

Several of the earlier writers mention what they considered to be a "*minor*" variety of the Lemon Daylily, but Philip Miller (*Gardeners Dictionary*, Edition 8, 1768) was the first to give specific rank to such a plant. He described a *Hemerocallis minor* as closely related to *H. flava* but as being different in having shorter leaves not more than half as wide as those of *H. flava* and scapes that rise only one and one-half feet. A type now in cultivation which corresponds closely to this description is shown in plate 2.

About the year 1798 a fulvous daylily found its way from the Orient into England and in 1804 it was listed under the name *Hemerocallis disticha* in a catalog of the plants then being grown in the Cambridge Botanical Garden. This type was evidently kept in cultivation for a time, for in 1823 a very good description and a colored plate of it were published. It had narrow petals and hence lacked fullness, and evidently it did not gain favor among gardeners. It seems that this plant did not become a parent of seedlings either hybrids or otherwise. It is clearly evident that this was a fulvous daylily of a wild type that may be included with the species *H. fulva* now known to be rather widely distributed in the wild in China and Japan.

The semi-dwarf daylily *H. Dumortierii* (plates 10 and 11) was first described in 1834 from plants that were obtained in Japan and grown in the Botanical Garden at Ghent, Belgium. In 1856 another semi-dwarf species was described under the name *H. Middendorffii* (plate 11) and ten years later plants of it were in culture in the Royal Botanic Garden in St. Petersburg.

Between the years 1860 and 1864 double-flowered fulvous daylilies (plate 7) in both pure green foliage and in white-striped or variegated foliage came into culture in Europe for the first time. These types had evidently long been cultivated in China and Japan where they had been observed and described by Kaempfer (in 1712) and by Thunberg (in 1784). These double-flowered forms are obviously cultivated clones to be included in the genus *H. fulva*.

Thus at the beginning of the year 1890 and after three

centuries had elapsed after the first descriptions of the *H. flava* and the *H. fulva* (clone Europa), only three new species *(H. minor, H. Dumortierii* and *H. Middendorffii)* and three additional clones of *H. fulva* ("*H. disticha*" and *H. fulva* Kwanso in both green and variegated foliage) had received prominent notice in Europe or America. Also during this time no hybrid or horticultural variety had appeared.

In the decade between 1890 and 1900 several distinctly new types of daylilies appeared in Europe or were definitely described for the first time. The yellow-flowered *H. Thunbergii* (plate 5) and the orange-fulvous *H. aurantiaca* (plate 8) were described in 1890 from plants growing in the Royal Botanic Gardens at Kew, England, but it seems that the former had been grown to some extent in Europe since as early as 1873. The so-called "*H. aurantiaca major*," noted in 1895, has orange-colored flowers of large size. The night-blooming *H. citrina* was sent from China into Italy about 1897 as was also the clone of the *H. fulva* which was called Maculata. Soon thereafter plants of *H. fulva* of wild origin came into culture in Italy under the names *H. fulva* Cypriana and *H. fulva* Hupehensis.

Since 1900 five more species of daylilies have been obtained from China and described. Of these the *H. Forrestii*, the *H. nana* (plates 4 and 26) and the *H. plicata* are dwarf or almost dwarf. The species *H. multiflora* (plate 9), which has numerous flowers to a scape and blooms in autumn after other species of daylilies are through flowering, was named in 1929 from wild plants that came from China. Also there have come to The New York Botanical Garden various somewhat new wild fulvous daylilies one of which has been called *H. fulva* var. *rosea*. The name *H. esculenta* was given in 1925 to a fulvous type growing in Japan but this has not yet come into culture in Europe or America, unless it is the same as some of the types otherwise named. Very recently the name *H. exaltata* has been given to wild plants from the Tobi Shima Islands of Japan.

The development of horticultural clones of daylilies by hybridization was begun about 1890 by Mr. George Yeld in England whose hybrid Apricot was mentioned in 1892. The first hybrids were obtained from the early-flowering species *H. flava, H. Dumortierii,* and *H. Middendorffii,* and probably also *H. minor.* In 1906 there were several hybrids known, including the excellent clones Apricot, Gold Dust, Estmere, Sovereign, Orangeman, and Tangerine. Various hybrids involving the summer-flowering types *H. Thunbergii, H. citrina, H. aurantiaca,* and *H. aurantiaca* Major were mentioned in 1900, 1903 and 1906, and hybrids between early-flowering and summer-flowering types soon appeared.

Hybrids with fulvous parentage were noted as early as 1899 (see Pioneer, in page 67) and 1903 (see Fulva-Cypriana, in page 50). Some were listed for the trade in 1903 (see Fulcitrina, in page 49), but hybrid fulvous daylilies of special merit have only appeared within the past few years, and some of these are the products of selective breeding continued through several hybrid generations.

The dwarf species *H. nana* is one of the parents of the clones Miniken, Moidore, and Nada. The species *H. Forrestii, H. nana,* and *H. plicata* are now being used in further hybridizations that should give new clones of value especially in dwarf plants. More than a thousand hybrids having the *H. multiflora* as a parent have been produced by the writer and already one of these has been named Bijou.

Thus the two old daylilies already in cultivation in Europe three and a half centuries ago have been augmented by new types obtained from the Orient until thirteen distinct species, or fourteen if we include the *H. esculenta,* have now been described. It is certain that various other types remain to be discovered, introduced into culture, and used in hybridizations.

Already about one hundred and fifty hybrid seedlings have been named as clones, propagated for culture, and mentioned in horticultural literature. The best of these are excellent plants of unusual charm. Several of the newer of the wild species and many of the best of the hybrid clones are of such recent introduction or origin that there has not been time for propagation and general distribution. At the present time many excellent daylilies are so new that they are rare plants not generally known to gardeners.

Through hybridization and selective breeding there has been a noteworthy improvement of daylilies as garden plants. At the present writing rapid strides are being made in the further development of rather distinctly new types which give diversity to the daylilies and add to their value as garden plants.

CHAPTER V

SPECIES OF DAYLILIES

Of the known daylilies at least thirteen distinct species are now to be recognized. In nearly all cases these were named and described from a few plants that were brought into cultivation in Europe or America. In certain cases these plants were from the wild; in other cases they were evidently plants selected or developed from wild stock and already in cultivation in the Orient. For several of the species all the plants studied at the time of the naming were of a single clone which may not be typical or even very representative of the wild members of the species. An extensive critical study has not been made of the wild daylilies of the Orient. No doubt various valid species remain to be discovered and named.

The species of daylilies may be classified according to various contrasts in structure, in habits of growth, in flower behavior, or in the coloring of the flowers. A recent classification with a key to the species of *Hemerocallis* by Dr. L. H. Bailey (*Gentes Herbarum* 2: 143–156. 1930) bases the primary grouping on whether the scapes are branched or unbranched. Further distinctions are based on stature, character of the perianth tube, color of flowers, flowering habits, and the shape and the width of the segments of the flowers. In the following key and descriptions attention is paid to these characteristics and also to the character of the roots, the branching habits of the underground stems, flowering habits, the behavior of the foliage in autumn, and the character of capsules.

Key to the Species of Hemerocallis

I. **Euhemera.** Scape forked or branched at the top except when flowers are solitary.

a. Scapes shorter than foliage or not greatly exceeding it; leaves narrow; flowers usually few, sometimes solitary, perianth tube short; plants dwarf or semi-dwarf; roots fleshy.

b. Bracts inconspicuous.

c. Leaves flat; flowers 1 to 3.
1. *H. nana.*

cc. Leaves usually folded; flowers as many as 5.
2. *H. plicata.*

bb. Bracts somewhat herbaceous; flowers as many as 4 or more. 3. *H. Forrestii.*

aa. Scapes taller than the foliage and usually much branched above.

b. Early flowering; flowers yellow or lemon yellow; capsule elliptical.

c. Roots fleshy and enlarged; with spreading rhizomes; capsule large and broadly elliptic; flowers strongly odorous. 4. *H. flava.*

cc. Roots slender-cylindrical and fibrous; crown branches compact, without spreading rhizomes; capsule narrow-elliptic. 5. *H. minor.*

bb. Flowering in mid-summer.

c. Flowers pale yellow; scapes stiffly erect; crown compact.

d. Main roots cylindrical and scarcely enlarged; flower-opening somewhat extended (night and day). 6. *H. Thunbergii.*

dd. Main roots decidedly fleshy but elongated and tapering; flowers nocturnal, perianth tube elongated and segments narrow.
7. *H. citrina.*

cc. Flowers with some shade of fulvous or red; flowering diurnal; foliage coarse; main roots enlarged; crown with spreading rhizomes.

d. Flowers usually strongly fulvous; foliage coarse, semi-evergreen; plants robust with scapes 4 to 5 feet. (See also "*H. esculenta,*" page 31).
8. *H. fulva.*

e. Perianth tube long and slender, and segments narrow. *H. fulva longituba.*

ee. Flower color rosy-red.
H. fulva rosea.

dd. Flowers with delicate over-cast of fulvous; foliage evergreen; scapes coarse, ascending rather than erect; semi-robust to about 3 feet.
9. *H. aurantiaca.*

ccc. Flowers orange; scapes erect, with coarse short branches rather closely grouped at the top; crown compact; roots only slightly fleshy.
10. *H. exaltata.*

bbb. Flowering in late summer and autumn; flowers orange, of small size; scapes much and finely branched; crown compact; main roots fleshy. 11. *H. multiflora.*

II. Dihemera. Scape unbranched; the 2–4 flowers sessile or nearly so, with bracts broad and overlapping. Early flowering (May and early June); crown compact; plants semi-dwarf, about 2 feet tall; foliage becoming dormant early in autumn.

a. Main roots very fleshy; scapes spreading rather than erect, and shorter than the leaves; flowers light orange, not opening widely; scapes and flower buds decidedly tinged with brownish red; capsule globose. 12. *H. Dumortierii.*

aa. Main roots slender cylindrical; flowers orange, segments broad-spatulate; flower buds and sepals of opened flowers noticeably ridged or pleated; scapes mostly slightly longer than leaves; capsule elliptical. 13. *H. Middendorffii.*

b. Scapes taller and more erect. *H. Middendorffii major.*

Description of Species[1]

1. *Hemerocallis nana* W. W. Smith and Forrest

This species was mentioned and a photograph of a wild plant was shown in the *Journal of the Royal Horticultural Society* in 1916 (**42**: figure 12). It was described in 1917 (*Notes Bot. Gard. Edinburgh* **10**: 39) and it was illustrated in color in 1923 (*Bot. Magazine* **148**: plate 8968). A typical plant of *Hemerocallis nana* received from the Gardens of the Royal Horticultural

[1] The plates 2, 3, 5, upper cut in 9, 10, lower cut in 12, 17 and 19 are reproduced to the same scale and one inch represents one foot of the plants. The several plants in the plate 26 are all shown in the same scale. In plates 35 and 36 the scale is six inches representing one foot. Thus these plates present plants in there relative statures.

Society in England and grown at The New York Botanical Garden is shown in plate 4 of this volume.

The plants of *H. nana* grow compactly with a crown of short and almost erect branches. Some of the main roots become somewhat enlarged and fleshy and, as far as the writer has observed, the fleshy part is at the end of a root and at some distance from the crown. For plants in culture, the leaves may be as much as 15 inches long and are expanded rather than plicate and longer than the scapes. *The scapes* are slender, bending outward, and usually they bear one flower. When there are two or more flowers the scape is branched. *The bracts* are inconspicuous and often there will be two to a scape even though there is but one flower. *The flowers* may have a spread of three or more inches; the segments are rather narrow; the tube is short and not sharply defined; the color on the inner face is a clear orange, but on the reverse there may be shades of reddish brown.

The photograph taken by Forrest and his herbarium material show plants with rather sparse foliage and short scapes. The same is true of specimens collected by F. J. Rock (his nos. 5321 and 9593) in 1922 and 1923 in Yunnan which appear to be of *H. nana*. In the herbarium specimens the leaves seem decidedly plicate, the tips of the leaves are often broken, and in the specimens collected by Forrest which the writer has seen, the tips of the leaves were evidently removed by some animal, with the result that the leaves appear to be shorter than the scapes. In comparison with these, the plants of this species grown in pots at The New York Botanical Garden (see plate 4) are larger with longer and broader leaves that are not plicate. It is to be expected that the plants which are grown in gardens or in pot culture will be taller and more lush than those plants which grow in the wild and especially when they are on poor soil in dry and rocky habitats.

This species somewhat resembles the *H. Dumortierii* in habits of growth and character of the flowers, but is less robust, the bracts are less conspicuous and the scapes are, when more than one-flowered, decidedly branched.

2. *Hemerocallis plicata* Stapf

This species was described as new by Stapf in 1923 *(Bot. Magazine* **148**: plate 8968) and as being different from *H. nana* especially in having folded leaves and more flowers to an inflorescence.

The New York Botanical Garden has obtained living plants bearing the name of this species from several sources. Few plants have bloomed well and the material has not been sufficient for adequate judgment of the specific distinctions. One plant received as *H. plicata* had a scape taller than the leaves and it was loosely branched and bore 8 flowers; in the face of the open flowers there was a faint but distinct halo of fulvous color; and the leaves were open and not plicate.

3. *Hemerocallis Forrestii* Diels

The first description of this species by Diels in 1912 *(Notes Bot. Gard. Edinburgh* **5**: 298) reports that the color of the flowers is deep reddish orange and there is the statement that this species is allied to *H. fulva* and especially to the so-called *H. fulva* var. *augustifolia* described by Baker. There has, however, been no trace of the epidermal fulvous pigment characteristic of *H. fulva* in any of the flowers of plants of this species which have bloomed at The New York Botanical Garden and which came under this name as living plants from The Royal Botanic Garden at Kew and from the gardens of the Royal Horticultural Society at Wisley, England. A colored plate and a description of one of these plants was published in 1930 *(Addisonia* **15**: plate 481).

Seedlings now being grown from seed[2] collected by J. F. Rock on the slopes of the Likiang Snow Range in China, and supposed to be of *H. Forrestii*, have fleshy roots and have been dormant in a greenhouse during winter.

The species *H. nana*, *H. plicata*, and *H. Forrestii* appear to be

[2] Supplied to the author by Professor T. H. Goodspeed, curator of the Botanical Garden of the University of California.

dwarf or nearly dwarf daylilies discovered in southwestern China by the botanical explorer Forrest. The descriptions and the herbarium specimens of wild plants indicate that in natural habitats many plants, at least of *H. nana,* are no taller than one foot. In culture in gardens or in pots placed in cold frames, plants are described as being as tall as 16 inches.

Plants of these species have been grown to some extent in botanical gardens and in private gardens in Europe and America. At The New York Botanical Garden, nearly all plants of these species which were planted in the open garden have died; most of those kept in a cold frame have lived but have not bloomed after the first year. This experience seems to indicate that these species may not be fully hardy in the northern part of the United States.

Mr. George Yeld has recently reported hybrids between *H. nana* and *H. flava,* two of which have been named Miniken and Moidore.

The writer has a considerable number of hybrids from plants received as *H. Forrestii, H. nana,* and *H. plicata* crossed with *H. flava, H. minor, H. Dumortierii,* and various seedlings having fulvous daylilies in their parentage, and one of these has been named the Nada Daylily.

These dwarf daylilies should be of value in further hybridizations and selective breeding in the development of dwarf or semi-dwarf clones comparable in flowering habits and flower colors to the best of the more robust clones now available for garden culture.

4. *Hemerocallis flava* Linn.

Lemon Daylily, Tall Yellow Daylily, or Custard Lily

The Lemon Daylily (plates 1, 2 and 26) has been a favorite garden flower in Europe for at least three and a half centuries and it remains today as one of the best of the daylilies, for there is no other yellow-flowered daylily of the same semi-robust stature that blooms as early in the season.

The flowers are a uniform lemon-chrome in color, strongly

and agreeably odorous, medium full, wide-spreading, of good size, and lasting well throughout the hours of daylight. Often the flowers remain fresh into a second day and then there will be two sets open for a time—behavior called "extended blooming" —(see plate 26). *The scapes* are ascending and almost erect, branching at the apex, and of a height of about three feet. *The foliage* is abundant, medium dark green in color, and the apex of the dome of leaves is about six inches below the flowers. *Rhizomes* spread rather widely and vigorously from a compact crown of many short branches, and many of the roots are fleshy. *Capsules* and *seeds* are readily formed to self-pollination, which is rather unusual for daylilies, but it is easier to propagate the plant by division. The capsules may be one and three-fourths inches in length by one and one-fourth inches in diameter; they are broadly elliptic in vertical outline, and almost triangular in median cross-section, and are the largest among the species of daylilies. The seeds are black, smooth, and irregularly rounded.

The Lemon Daylily is the plant that was mentioned in botanical literature as early as 1570 (in *Historia* by Pena and Lobel) under the name *Asphodelus luteus liliflorus.* It remained in cultivation and 192 years later it received from Linnaeus (in 1762) its modern botanical name *Hemerocallis flava.* There are many references to this daylily in horticultural and botanical literature. Several colored plates showing it have appeared, the latest being in *Addisonia,* **14**: plate 457, here reproduced in plate 1.

There are several different clones in cultivation under the name *H. flava* which differ somewhat from the type, in stature, size of flowers, habits of growth, and shape of capsules. One of these clones has somewhat smaller flowers, scapes and foliage that are more stiffly erect, and capsules that are more blunt and slightly beaked.

5. *Hemerocallis minor* Miller

Grass-leaved Daylily

There are various low-growing daylilies cultivated under the names *H. minor, H. graminea, H. gracilis,* and *H. graminifolia.*

Some of these are obviously either variations of *H. Dumortierii* or hybrids with this species as one of the parents, but some of them are of a type that is distinct from the *H. flava* and that conforms closely to the first but meager description of *H. minor* by Miller in 1768. This type is illustrated in color with discussion and description in *Addisonia* (**14**: plate 458. 1929). A photograph of a plant is here shown in plate 2.

The flowers are, on the inner face, uniformly of a lemon-chrome shade of yellow, the perianth tube is greenish, and the outside of the sepals is tinged with brownish red. *The scapes* are slender, ascending about two feet tall, and somewhat short-branching above. *The foliage* is composed of slender narrow leaves as long as 15 to 18 inches, but as they are weakly ascending the mound of foliage stands well below the flowers. The foliage dies completely to the ground early in autumn and all buds become dormant. *The capsule* is narrow elliptic in outline, somewhat triangular in cross-section, and about one and one-half inches in length, and its seeds are about one-eighth inch in length, of the smallest size known for any species of *Hemerocallis*. *The flowering* is in early spring, beginning about ten days later than the *H. flava*. *The crown* is extremely compact with short erect branches, and rhizomes are lacking. *The roots* are slender cylindrical and not fleshy, with numerous fibrous laterals, and they are flesh-brown in color.

Plants conforming closely to the above description have been obtained from various sources, but some of them have had somewhat taller flower scapes.

This species is quite distinct from the *H. flava*. It is smaller in every feature except size of flower; its foliage dies much earlier in autumn; it is more compact in the crown; the roots are smaller, finer, and not fleshy; the capsule is more slender and the seeds are much smaller.

The true Grass-leaved Daylily is seldom seen in flower gardens. Its flowers are abundant and of good size, color, and lasting quality. Its season of bloom overlaps that of the Lemon

Daylily, but the marked differences in stature and character of foliage give it distinctive value.

6. *Hemerocallis Thunbergii* Baker

Thunberg's Daylily, Late Yellow Daylily

A daylily was mentioned under the name *Hemerocallis Thunbergii* by Peter Barr in 1873 (*The Garden* **4**: 132) as a plant that starts to flower somewhat later than the *H. fulva* (The Europa Daylily), has flowers a clear beautiful yellow in color, and is three feet tall. This plant was first listed for sale in the catalog of Barr and Sugden in 1873. A letter from Barr and Sons received in 1933 states that this plant was offered in each catalog of the firm issued yearly from 1873 to 1890.

A somewhat detailed description of this species which appeared in July 1890 (*Gard. Chr.* **8**: 95) was based on plants then being grown in the Royal Botanic Gardens at Kew, England. Baker applied the name as "*Hemerocallis Thunbergii* Baker Hort.," which indicates that he was aware that this name was already in use for this plant in horticultural circles. It happens that one year earlier Focke briefly described (*Abhandl. nat. Vereine z. Bremen* **10**: 156–158. 1899), under the name *H. Serotina*, a summer-flowering yellow-flowered daylily which was then growing in the Botanic Garden at Bremen, Germany, and which had come from a nursery in Germany under the name *H. Dumortierii.* It appears that there are no herbarium specimens, drawings, or illustrations of Focke's plant, and also that this particular plant has not been continued in cultivation at least under this name even at Bremen or Hamburg. On the other hand the plants at Kew were propagated and widely distributed, and have remained in continuous culture under the name *H. Thunbergii.* A colored plate showing a flower and a capsule of what is believed to be the clone of this plant was published in *Addisonia* (**14**: plate 459. 1929). A photograph of a plant is shown in plate 5 of this volume.

Plants of Thunberg's Daylily, of the clone widely cultivated and believed to be that named by Baker, have a robust and compact habit of growth and are strongly spreading in the crown by short erect branches. *The roots* are mostly slender-cylindrical but occasionally some of the roots are somewhat enlarged and fleshy. *The foliage* is medium dark green and ascending-spreading to a general level of about thirty inches, and it dies in late autumn, usually not until after frost. *The scapes* are numerous, slender, stiffly erect to a height of about forty-five inches, and they are well-branched above. *The flowers* are lemon-yellow in color with the tube and the outside of the sepals strongly tinged with green; they have a spread of about three inches and they tend to fade and wilt in the afternoon during hot sunny weather. *Flowering* is in midsummer; in New York it blooms in July along with the Europa Daylily and after plants of *H. flava* and *H. minor* have ceased to bloom. *The capsule* is broadly blunt at the apex, almost truncate, and much smaller than the capsule of *H. flava.*

The clone of *H. Thunbergii* in general culture is evidently a selection from a rather variable wild species that grows in the Orient. The writer has plants of this species collected wild in northern Japan which are later in season of flowering than are plants of the type in general culture since 1873. There are now several clones in culture which differ in minor characteristics and which are either seedlings of the clone originally described, or later importations, or possibly hybrids. In the original clone the basal and underground portion of the leaves is white. There are several clones somewhat similar to *H. Thunbergii* that have pink colors in the base of the leaves. Some of these may be second generation hybrids of this species crossed with *H. citrina* or with some other type.

Thunberg's Daylily has an excellent robust habit, attractive dark green foliage, and an abundance of flowers. It is to be classed as a good garden plant for bloom in mid-summer. It has been used rather extensively in hybridizations. In size of flowers and in richness and purity of yellow coloring it is perhaps surpassed or at least supplemented by various of the new hybrids. Thunberg's Daylily is rather widely known in American gardens.

7. *Hemerocallis citrina* Baroni

Citron Daylily, Long Yellow Daylily

The Citron Daylily is a type of distinctive characteristics. *The flowers* are night-blooming or nocturnal (see plate 29); they begin to open shortly before sunset, are widely open during the night, and they usually close early in the following forenoon especially on warm sunny days. They are of large size with a long tube, but the segments are narrow. The color is pale lemon-yellow; the sepals are greenish on the back and purplish at the tips, a feature especially noticeable in the bud. The flowers are fragrant and the period of blooming is in midsummer. *The foliage* is coarse, vigorous in growth, as long as 40 inches, decidedly erect but often bending or even breaking abruptly. Its color during summer is dark green, but in autumn it dies quickly and for a time is conspicuously yellowish brown. The base of the leaves in the soil is pink or almost bright red. *The scapes* are stiffly erect, about forty-five inches tall, and much branched near the apex, bearing numerous flowers. The writer has counted as many as 64 flower buds to a single scape. *The capsules* are usually about one inch in length, obovate, and indented and purplish at the apex. *The crown* (see plate 36) is compact and without spreading rhizomes. Of the main roots many are long and slender of a diameter of about 3/16 inch but some are spindle-shaped and enlarged to a diameter of about ½ inch. The younger roots are orange in color and the older main roots are almost brown.

The Citron Daylily has an excellent and robust habit of growth and an abundance of attractive dark green foliage, but because of the night-blooming habit and the narrow segments of the flowers it is not valuable for garden use. This species has been much hybridized with various other daylilies and especially with

H. Thunbergii. Some of the seedlings, as the Ophir Daylily, far surpass the parent in having large full flowers of good day-blooming habit and much richer color.

Several different clones are being distributed under the name *H. citrina* which differ somewhat, especially in the height of the scapes and in the size of the flowers. The plants described above, and also illustrated in *Addisonia* (**16**: plate 482. 1930), came directly from the nursery of Willy Müller in Naples, Italy, and are said to be of the clone originally described and distributed to the trade.

8. *Hemerocallis fulva* Linn.

Fulvous or Tawny Daylily

There are several cultivated clones and various wild types or varieties that are to be included under the specific name *Hemerocallis fulva.*

The clone Europa (plate 3). The oldest and the best-known of the fulvous daylilies is the one commonly known as *Hemerocallis fulva* L. This single-flowered daylily was described under the name *Liriosphodelus phoeniceus* by Lobel in 1576 (*Historia*) as having cinnabar-red coloring in the flowers and as being very distinct from the yellow-flowered daylily (*H. flava*), which was then also in cultivation in Europe. In 1601, Clusius (*Plantarum Historia*) states that this plant was being grown in many gardens throughout Austria and Germany. Nearly two hundred years later, Linnaeus (1753) considered this daylily a hybrid, but a few years afterward (*Species Plantarum*, ed. 2, 1762) he gave to it specific rank with the name *Hemerocallis fulva.*

But the plants of this particular daylily do not produce seeds to any kind of pollination possible for them alone. They have always been propagated solely by vegetative divisions and they are all merely branches derived from one original seedling. They constitute a clone. It has been suggested by the writer (*Jour. N. Y. Bot. Garden* **30**: 129–136. 1929) that the horticultural name "Europa Daylily" be used to designate this daylily as a horticultural clone that is distinct from various others of the species.

It is now known that this particular clone is a triploid; that is, there are three sets of 11 chromosomes each ($3n=33$) in its cells instead of the two sets ($2n=22$) found in wild plants of the species. This condition leads to many irregularities in sporogenesis and the plants are almost completely sterile, a condition frequently seen in triploids. Also there is complete self-incompatibility for the pollen which is viable, a condition that is very general among daylilies. While seeds have been obtained with the Europa Daylily as a parent in hybridizations, seeds to self-pollination are, evidently, not possible.

The Europa Daylily probably arose as a single aberrant seedling, either wild or in garden culture. Possibly the fullness of its flowers and the somewhat bold pattern of their coloring were outstanding qualities that long ago attracted the attention of some Oriental gardener. The plant happened also to have the habit of spreading vigorously by rhizomes and this made vegetative propagation easy and has maintained the individual character of the original seedling throughout several centuries of garden culture. This clone remains today in vigorous growth; a demonstration that long-continued asexual reproduction does not of itself necessarily reduce vigor and lead to degeneration. We may perhaps assume that the Daylily Europa had its origin in the Orient together with the Lemon Daylily (*H. flava*). How and when these two found their way into garden culture in Europe, where they were reported in 1567, is a matter of conjecture.

A plant of the Europa Daylily is one of the most robust of daylilies (plate 3). It extends itself vigorously by coarse widely spreading rhizomes (plate 35). *The roots* are numerous and many of them become enlarged and fleshy. *The foliage* is light green, rather coarse, strongly distichous in arrangement, and it forms a dome about three feet in height. In coarseness of foliage it is surpassed among the older daylilies only by the double-flowered form. The older leaves die in autumn but younger leaves continue to appear which remain somewhat green until heavy frosts. *The scapes* are coarse and strong, stiffly erect to a height of about 50 inches, and they are branched at the summit bearing as many as 15 to 20 flowers. *The flowers* have a fulvous overcast of color in the outer zone of the open flower with reticulated veins of darker shades. An arching mid-zone of darker shade in the petals is a conspicuous feature. The throat of the flower is orange only. The petals are rather thin, slightly wavy along the margin, and of delicate texture; yet they retain form and color well during the day. The segments are rather broad and overlapping, giving a full flower. The flowers are strictly day-blooming; they open after daylight and close about sunset. The season of blooming is in July. *The capsule,* produced only rarely and to the compatible fertilizations of certain cross-pollinations, is about one inch in length, broadly ovate, with the apex truncate and indented.

The persistent self-unfruitfulness of the entire clone of the Europa Daylily makes it impossible to obtain selfed seedlings. It is only within very recent years that the Europa Daylily has been used successfully in hybridization with other daylilies.

Double-flowered Fulvous Daylilies (plate 7) exist both with green foliage and with white-striped variegated foliage. They all closely resemble the Europa Daylily in the color of the flowers, in habits of growth, in the diurnal habit of flowering, and in the season of bloom which is in midsummer. The first of these to be introduced into Europe was diplayed under the name "*Hemerocallis disticha flore pleno*" by Veitch and Son before the Royal Horticultural Society in 1860 (*Gard. Chr.* for 1860, page 482) and a year later a colored plate was published (*The Floral Magazine* **1**: plate 13) which shows a flower that was much doubled. A few years later mention was made of a "*Hemerocallis Kwanso foliis variegatis*" (*Gard. Chr.* 1864, page 654) which had been introduced directly from Japan by von Siebold. This was soon illustrated in a colored plate (*Gartenflora* **15**: plate 500. 1866) which shows the white-striped foliage and a flower somewhat less double than that of the plant already introduced by Veitch and Son. In the *Gardeners' Chronicle* in 1867 (page 292) this variegated type is called "*Hemerocallis Kwanso flore-pleno*." Thus it appears that the name "Kwanso" was first used for a daylily that was both variegated and double-flowered.

Plants of the variegated double-flowered type have been secured from several sources for culture in The New York Botanical Garden. The variegation is evidently of the chimeral type, an association of green and white cells, and the plants frequently produce all-green branches and offsets which continue as purely green plants. Hence it may well be that some of the double-flowered plants with all-green foliage now in cultivation arose from the variegated Kwanso Daylily.

The New York Botanical Garden has also obtained entirely green-leaved plants under the names Kwanso and Flore-Pleno from nurserymen, from botanical gardens, and from various localities in China and Japan. These have been grown side by side for comparison and study. There seems to be no noticeable difference in the color of the flowers and in the various aspects of the habit of growth. Some plants, however, have all flowers very double, while other plants have semi-double flowers. For certain of these plants various degrees of doubleness may be found on the same plant but never has a flower had a perfect pistil.

The propagation of the double-flowered types is solely by division, for the pistils of the flowers are transformed into a column of petals and the formation of fruit is not possible. Stamens or anthers are usually present but the pollen is mostly aborted. All of the double-flowered plants thus far studied are triploids.

Of the origin of the double-flowered type there is no record. It was in existence in Japan in 1712 and it is known to be now rather widely distributed in Japan and to some extent also in China, both in culture and as an apparent escape, evidently quite as the Europa Daylily now exists in such old-settled areas as Long Island, about abandoned homesites, along roadsides, and wherever the activities of man have given the plant a chance to spread vegetatively. The very close relationship between the double-flowered types Kwanso, Flore-Pleno, Variegated, and the single-flowered Europa Daylily is obvious. All are triploids, and they are very similar in flower-colors and habits of growth, and all are strictly diurnal in flowering habit.

When plants of the Europa Daylily are grown beside plants having double flowers the former are somewhat earlier to bloom, have foliage somewhat less coarse and the scapes are taller. The color of the flowers is almost the same. The zone or eye spot is, however, less developed in the smaller and inner accessory segments of the double flowers than in their more primary segments and in the petals of the single-flowered Europa Daylily.

The double-flowered daylilies have not become popular garden flowers. To many persons the flowers seem monstrous, coarse, and lacking in pleasing symmetry. The Variegated Kwanso is seldom grown in American gardens. A single-flowered type with variegated foliage has been mentioned in the literature but this has never been seen by the writer nor has it been learned where it may be obtained.

Hemerocallis disticha Donn. Evidently no fulvous daylily other than the clone Europa found its way into Europe until about 1798 when the "*Hemerocallis disticha*" was obtained from China. The descriptions and the colored plate (*British Flower Garden*, plate 28, by Sweet) of this plant make it clear that it was a fulvous daylily with elongated perianth tube and narrow segments, which made it appear to be quite distinct from the Europa Daylily. It remained in cultivation, at least for some time.

Hemerocallis longituba Miquel. In 1867 the Dutch botanist Miquel described certain herbarium specimens as a new species *Hemerocallis longituba*. The flowers had a long perianth tube, the color was supposed to be fulvous.

Hemerocallis fulva angustifolia Baker. A daylily that was considered to belong with the species *H. fulva* was described under the varietal name *angustifolia* in 1871 by Baker (*Jour.*

Linn. Soc. **11**: 359). Baker describes his plants as very small, with scapes scarcely a foot tall, and with leaves only 12 to 18 inches long and only 2 to 4 lines wide. The segments of the flowers are described as narrow and acute; but there is no definite mention of color. It is of special interest to note that this description was based on dried specimens which, it is stated, came from Khasia, India, from Guriev, which is near the extreme northwestern side of the Caspian Sea, and from Karabagh, which is farther south and in Caucasia. It seems that this form with narrow leaves may be related to one of the types recently described as *H. Forrestii*, *H. nana*, or *H. plicata*, or that it may belong with a new species. At least Baker's plants may be disregarded as a type to be included with the *H. fulva* of Linnaeus or as closely related to it.

H. fulva longituba Maximowicz. The Russian botanist Maximowicz described in 1885 (*Gartenflora* **34**: 98. plate 1187) and illustrated with a colored plate certain daylilies of a type obtained from the wild in the Hakone Mts. of Japan and said also to be in cultivation in Japan. The flowers are described as orange-yellow with slight fulvous tinges and as having the perianth-tube long and narrow. This type is described as different from the *H. fulva* of Linnaeus (the clone Europa) in having narrower leaves and also flowers with less fulvous color and a longer perianth-tube. The description by Maximowicz is followed by a note by E. Regel, Director of the Botanical Garden in St. Petersburg, stating that in good garden soil these wild plants differ from the old form of *H. fulva* chiefly in having a long perianth-tube.

Hemerocallis fulva clone Maculata. The clone Maculata is similar to the Europa Daylily. The coloring of the flowers is only slightly different; the fulvous shades in the outer half of the opened flower are slightly paler and the arching band across the mid-section of the petals is slightly darker. The flowers are larger than those of the Europa Daylily and the petals are of a different shape. The plants are somewhat later in the period of blooming, but they are very similar in habit of growth except

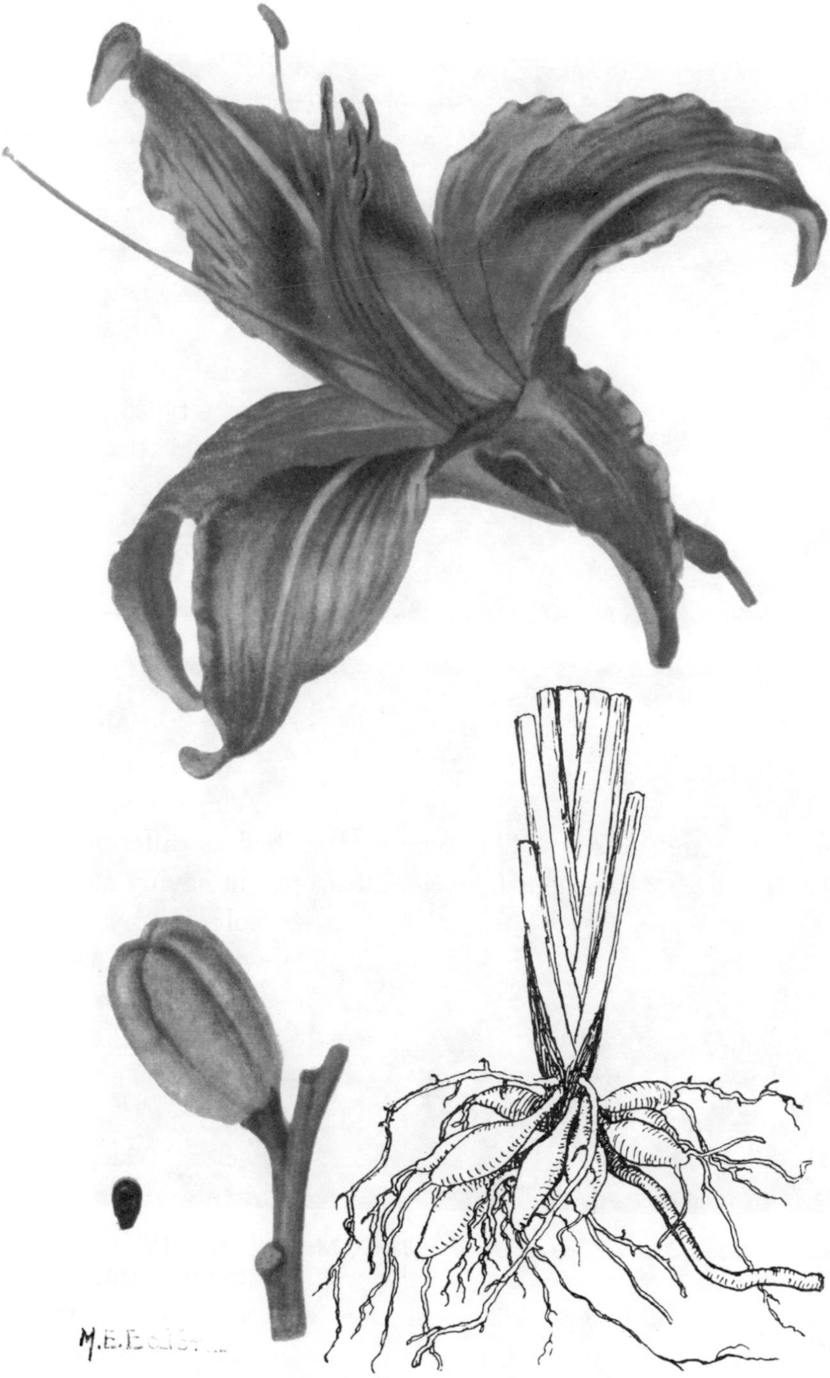

Plate 6. The Maculata Daylily (*H. fulva* clone Maculata)

Plate 7. *Above*, double-flowered Daylily. *Below*, Margaret Perry Daylily

that the scapes are slightly shorter. A colored plate showing a flower and a capsule of this clone, here seen in plate 6, was published in *Addisonia* (**14**: plate 460) with a description and a statement of the history of this plant. All the plants of this clone are self-fruitless and they set no seed to pollination among themselves. They are also triploid and decidedly sterile, but have been utilized in hybridization.

In 1903 Sprenger reported (*Gard. Chr.* **34**: 122) that he had obtained hybrids with *H. fulva* clone Maculata as a pollen parent on *H. citrina* and on *H. aurantiaca* clone Major (see note on Fulcitrina in Chapter VI).

Hemerocallis fulva clone Hupehensis. This clone was derived from a seedling plant grown by C. Sprenger in Naples, Italy from seed collected by Padre Cypriani in Hupeh, China. The first published mention of this clone appeared in 1906 (*Gard. Chr.* **40**: 158) when the flower is described as "reflexed, undulating, bright coppery red, with yellow throat."

Hemerocallis fulva clone Cypriani. This clone has the same source and history as clone Hupehensis. Willy Müller described (*Gard. Chr.* **40**: 159. 1906) the flowers as "coppery red with a golden center and a well marked golden line down the middle of the petals. The form is gracefully reflexed." This and the clone Hupehensis are fulvous daylilies very similar to various wild seedlings which the writer has grown. They have no special merit as garden plants.

Fulvous Daylilies in the Literature of Oriental Plants. Various botanical treatments by Japanese botanists and by Europeans who have observed or collected plants in Japan and China make mention of fulvous daylilies. In some cases the single-flowered types of the fulvous daylilies, other than the *H. aurantiaca* which will be discussed later, are included in the name *Hemerocallis fulva*, but by some writers they are all called *H. disticha* and in a few instances there is reference to *H. fulva* var. *longituba.*

In none of these descriptions and lists is there a critical discussion of the types and variations that were observed, and adequate descriptions and comparisons of the cultivated and the wild types are not made.

Fulvous Daylilies of Wild Origin have been obtained from various localities in Japan and China and grown at The New York Botanical Garden. The writer is especially indebted to Dr. A. N. Steward for plants of this type from China and to Mr. T. Susa for plants from Japan. All these plants are very much alike in general habit of growth. The leaves are light green, medium coarse, strongly distichous, and ascending-curving. The scapes stand at a height of about four feet. Compared with the Europa Daylily they have foliage that is usually less robust. Some have scapes that are shorter, others have scapes that are taller. There is, however, the same feature of spreading rhizomes and the capsules are of the same type.

In respect to the precise character of the flowers of these plants there is much variation. All have some shade or degree of fulvous red in the coloring of the face of the flower and in most cases there is a somewhat darker zone just outside of the throat of the flower. Some of the plants from Japan have the duller and more brownish shades; some of those from Kuling, China have bright shades of pink and red, and to this type the varietal name *Hemerocallis fulva* var. *rosea* has been given (*Addisonia* **15**: plate 484. 1930). For many of these, the flowers have a long perinanth-tube and the segments are long and narrow and for this type the most proper botanical name is *H. fulva* var. *longituba* Maxim.

Several groups of fulvous daylilies obtained from Korea and northern Japan are taller and more robust than the Europa Daylily and they bloom later in summer. One group has continued in flower from August until severe killing temperatures occur in November.

Possibly a more complete knowledge of the natural distribution of the various types of fulvous daylilies will reveal that there are readily two or more distinct species which are more or less intermingled and hybridized in certain areas. At the present time it seems best to include the variations discussed above, both of the wild and of the cultivated plants, in the one species *H. fulva* L., of which the clone Europa is the historical type.

Some of the variations among these daylilies of the species *H. fulva* are certain to be of value in culture and in the breeding for new horticultural types. Already in the breeding work at The New York Botanical Garden the plants with pink and red colorings in the flowers have been used in selective breeding, and seedlings have been obtained that are of sprightly and pleasing shades of dark red, purplish red, bright red, and of rosy pink forming distinctly new horticultural races. Several of the best of these seedlings are being propagated as clones for garden culture, and several are described in the next chapter.

Hemerocallis esculenta. The name *Hemerocallis esculenta* was used by Koidzumi (*Bot. Mag. Tokyo* **39**: 28. 1925) in describing a daylily with pale red-yellow flowers, oblong rather than narrow segments, and scapes that are 90 cm. tall. In the color of the flowers this plant seems to be a fulvous daylily. Yet Koidzumi states that it is allied to the *H. Thunbergii,* which it may be noted, has no element of red coloring in the face of the flowers. The writer has not seen living plants of this type and hence is not able to compare it with the variations of *H. fulva* here mentioned or to give critical judgment of its status, but it seems probable that this plant is not different from various wild plants from Japan which are here considered as *H. fulva.*

9. *Hemerocallis aurantiaca* Baker

Orange-Fulvous Daylily

The name *Hemerocallis aurantiaca* was given by Baker in 1890 (*Gard. Chr.* **68**: 94) to a plant that was then growing in the Royal Botanic Gardens at Kew, England. The origin of this plant was not definitely known except that it was believed that it had been received from Japan. This plant was propagated by division to give a clone of plants now in cultivation in Europe and America under the name *H. aurantiaca.* In the *Somoku-Dzusetsu,* an early Japanese treatise on plants, there is an uncolored plate of a daylily which was later considered by Makino (3rd Edition of *Somoku* **6**: plate 13) to belong with the *H. aurantiaca* and it is stated that this species grows wild in the region of Mt. Ibuki. It is, however, not certain that the clone described by Baker is typical of a wild type that exists in Japan. Baker's plant may even be of horticultural origin. However, it may be considered the type of a species as he named it until there is definite knowledge otherwise.

The plant stands with scapes about 3 feet high and extending well above the mound of leaves. *The foliage* is medium coarse, strongly distichous, stiffly recurving, and decidedly evergreen in that it remains green and growing until winter ensues. These clusters of leaves suffer somewhat from winter injury but with the coming of warm weather in spring the plant soon recovers and so can be classed as hardy about New York City. In the tropics this daylily and certain of its hybrids remain green and growing throughout the year. *The scapes* are coarse, ascending rather than erect, coarsely branched above, and there are nodes without branches which bear conspicuous leaf-like bracts. *The flowers* (plate 7) are either sessile or on short stout pedicels. The open flower has a spread of about five inches. The segments are stiffly recurving, of firm texture, and those on the lower side of the flower are less recurving, giving to a flower the appearance of being less widely open than flowers of other species excepting the *H. Dumortierii.* In the throat the color of the flower is orange, but outside of this area the petals and sepals are delicately tinged with English red, and hence this type is to be classed as a fulvous daylily. It is, however, very distinct from the various types of *H. fulva.* Its scapes are lower; the foliage is darker green and more evergreen; the flowers are only pale fulvous, without reticulations, less widely open and the segments are less broad. The season of bloom is in July at the time when the Europa Daylily is in flower.

A good colored illustration of the flower and capsule believed to be of the clone which was named *H. aurantiaca* by Baker is shown in *Addisonia* **14**: plate 461. Several clones somewhat

Plate 8. *Above, Hemerocallis aurantiaca* clone Major and *H. aurantiaca. Below*, Cinnabar Daylily

Plate 9. Plant and flowers of *H. multiflora*

different from this one and of uncertain origin are sometimes called *H. aurantiaca.*

The so-called "*H. aurantiaca major*" (see plate 8) is very similar to the *H. aurantiaca* in habits of growth, characters of foliage and scapes, and season of flowering and the identity of the two is sometimes confused in horticultural literature, but the flowers of the latter are much larger and have no trace of fulvous coloring and the plant is less hardy. A more complete discussion by the writers of the *H. aurantiaca* and the *H. aurantiaca* Major was published in 1933 (*New Flora and Silva* **5**: 187–192).

10. *Hemerocallis exaltata* Stout

This species has recently been described (*Addisonia* **18**: plate 595. 1934) from living plants obtained through the kindness of Mr. T. Susa and collected wild on the Tobi Shima Islands off the west coast of Japan. *The plant* is robust, the mound of coarse foliage reaching a height of about 30 inches and the scapes a height of from 4 to 5 feet. *The crown* is compact without spreading rhizomes. *The main roots* are mostly slender-cylindrical but a few are somewhat enlarged. *The scapes* are stiffly erect, with coarse short branches at the extreme top. *The flowers* are light orange in color, spreading to a width of about 4 inches, rather full, the petals somewhat spatulate in shape, and widely open during daylight. The period of flowering is in late June and July. *The capsules* are elliptic in outline, as much as 1½ inches long, and noticeably corrugated with numerous short ridges.

Hemerocallis exaltata is very distinct from the other species of daylilies. Its flowers and capsules resemble those of *H. Middendorffii* but the plant is much more robust and the scapes are decidedly branched, although the branches are rather short and coarse.

The plants of this species are not especially attractive as garden plants; the foliage is somewhat lax and the flowers rather small and the inflorescence compact in relation to the robust habit of the plant. Hybrids between this species and various other daylilies are being grown.

11. *Hemerocallis multiflora* Stout

The Many-flowered Daylily

This daylily (plate 9) was first described in 1929 (*Addisonia* 14: plate 464) from living plants which were found growing wild at Ki Kung Shan, Honan, China by Dr. Albert N. Steward and sent by him to The New York Botanical Garden. *The crown* branches are compact without spreading rhizomes. *The roots* are fleshy with rather short enlargements. *The foliage* is ascending-arching to a general level of about twenty inches, is medium fine, and dies in late autumn after freezing temperatures but remains erect for a time changing to brown shades of color. *The scapes* are slender, in most plants ascending-bending, and much and finely branched, bearing in the entire season of bloom numerous flowers. *The flowers* are spreading to a width of about three inches, the color is a shade of orange that approaches "chrome," the perianth tube is tinged with green and the back of the sepals is slightly brownish red. Two of the plants originally obtained from China bloom during July and August but the others flower from late in August until heavy freezing temperatures occur, sometimes as late as in November. *The capsules* are seldom more than an inch in length and ovoid or obovoid in shape, but with seeds relatively large.

This species is itself not especially valuable as a garden plant. Although it has a long season of flowering the flowers are not noticeably numerous on a plant during any one day. It is being employed in extensive hybridizations with other daylilies in the effort to utilize its desirable characteristics such as (a) long period of flowering (b), numerous flowers to a scape, and (c) late summer and autumn flowering in obtaining hybrids of value for garden culture. One of these hybrids has been named Bijou.

12. *Hemerocallis Dumortierii* Morren

Dumortier's Daylily (plates 10, 11, and 36) is one of the earliest of daylilies to bloom in spring. *The plants* usually stand less than two feet tall. *The stems* branch compactly in the crown and spreading rhizomes are lacking. *The roots* are conspicuously enlarged. *The foliage* is rather stiffly ascending-spreading and the leaves are nearly an inch in width, appearing somewhat coarse for the stature of the plant. *The scapes* are unbranched, slender, usually shorter than the leaves, and not erect but merely ascending at an angle, and mostly disposed around the periphery of the mound of foliage. *The flowers* are sessile or on short pedicles, with usually two to four flowers compacted into a close inflorescence with overlapping basal bracts of which the lowest one is nearly two inches in length and accuminate. The flower buds are strongly tinged with brownish red which persists on the back of the sepals after the flower is open. The petals are about two inches long and one-half inch in greatest width, and the sepals are smaller, and in opening the segments are merely spreading and not recurving, hence the flower is not widely open. The color of the inner surface of the flower is orange without any trace of fulvous tints. *The capsules* when well-formed are at least an inch in length and decidedly globose in shape. An excellent colored plate of this species published in *Addisonia* (plate 462, 1929) is here reproduced in plate 11.

Living plants of *H. Dumortierii* were sent by M. von Siebold from Japan to the Botanical Garden at Ghent where they first flowered in 1832. Evidently this original type of the species has been kept in cultivation to the present time largely by vegetative propagation. Wild plants obtained by the writer from northern Japan are very similar to the clone described above except that some of the plants have flowers paler in color.

Several clones in cultivation under the names *H. rutilens*, *H. Sieboldii*, and even *H. minor* are to be included in the species *H. Dumortierii* or as somewhat aberrant forms of it. Some of these are not more than a foot in height and are to be classed as truly dwarf (see plate 27). Whether these have originated from cultivated types or represent wild types is not known.

This species is surpassed in vigor and in the size and the abundance of flowers by various of the hybrid offspring such as

Gold Dust, Sovereign, Estmere, and Orangeman which are much more showy as garden plants.

13. *Hemerocallis Middendorffii* Trautvetter and Meyer

The first mention of Middendorff's Daylily, or the Amur Daylily, was published in 1856 (*Florula Ochotensis,* page 94) and referred to herbarium specimens collected by the botanist Middendorff in the Amur Region. Ten years later living plants of this species were being grown in the Royal Botanic Garden at St. Petersburg. *Plants* (plates 10 and 36) of this daylily grow compactly in the crown, are without spreading rhizomes, and the roots are cylindrical, fibrous, and not fleshy. *The foliage* is medium dark green in color, seldom more than two feet long or more than three-fourths inch in width. *The scapes* are unbranched, rather upright, and slightly taller than the foliage. *The flowers* are closely clustered at the apex of the unbranched scape, with the lower part almost enclosed in a broad bract that is rather short and blunt. The flower bud is decidedly ridged or pleated. The flower opens widely to a spread of about three inches; the petals are noticeably spatulate in shape; and the color is a uniform orange. *The capsules* are triangular in cross-section and elliptic in longitudinal outline, somewhat similar in general shape to the capsules of *H. flava* and *H. minor,* but the surface is more or less corrugated with lateral ridges. A colored plate showing the main characteristics of this species was published in *Addisonia* (**14**: plate 453. 1929).

This species has sometimes been confused with Dumortier's Daylily (see discussion for Flavo-citrina on page 48). Both have a low-growing habit and unbranched scapes and both are early-flowering. But the shapes of the petals and of the capsules are very different and the scapes of the Amur Daylily are taller, more erect, and they carry the flowers to a level slightly above the leaves, and the main roots are slender-cylindrical and not fleshy.

Wild plants have been obtained from Japan which are probably of this species but are somewhat different from the older

Plate 10. *Above, Hemerocallis Middendorffii. Below, Hemerocallis Dumortierii*

Plate 11. Dumortier's Daylily (*H. Dumortierii*)

type in culture. Some have slightly paler flowers; some have taller and more erect scapes more like the *H. Middendorffii major;* for some the flowers number as many as ten to a scape, and at least some of the flowers have a distinct pedicel.

The *H. Middendorffii major* is somewhat more robust and the flowers are more numerous on a scape but otherwise it is almost identical with the type described above.

CHAPTER VI

THE HORTICULTURAL CLONES OF DAYLILIES

THIS alphabetical list includes those daylilies which, it is certain, do not definitely belong to any wild species. In nearly all cases they are known to be hybrids of horticultural origin and in most cases they have been given horticultural names.

The descriptions are mostly brief and chiefly confined to the most important characteristics. When the data are available, mention is made of the origin, the approximate year of introduction, and the important references to literature and illustrations. In various cases it is obvious that two or more somewhat different clones are being cultivated and distributed under one name. This situation, rather frequent in horticulture, necessarily leads to more or less uncertainty regarding the identification of the clone that was first named.

In considering these descriptions, it is to be recognized that there is some variation in the vigor and height of plants owing to conditions of culture and propagation. It takes several years for a small division to become well-established, and the total number of flowers and the extent of the season of flowering varies accordingly. Also the precise period of blooming will differ according to latitude, and dates of blooming in England and in the region about New York City will not coincide.

For all the varieties which the writer has not seen in flower or has seen only as small plants no responsibility is assumed either for the accuracy or for the adequacy of the descriptions quoted.

Various individuals, nursery firms, and institutions are mentioned in connection with the descriptions. Certain abbreviations are employed especially for various publications frequently referred to and these are explained in the Appendix.

Alphabetical List of Clonal Varieties

AJAX. About 30 inches tall; foliage evergreen, rather coarse; scapes coarse, ascending. Flowers cadmium-yellow with faint fulvous tinge when flowers first open; buds brownish red. Produced by Willy Müller at Naples, Italy; offered to trade in 1908; said to be hybrid of "*H. aurantiaca major*" × *H. citrina*; has characters which strongly resemble *H. Dumortierii*, but is more robust. Blooms chiefly in June, starting soon after the earliest of daylilies. Well-established plants are very floriferous.

AMARYLLIS. Mentioned by Mrs. Thomas Nesmith in 1932 (*Hort.* **10**: 292); 3 ft. tall; large flower, soft yellow, tipped with deeper color; flowering in July. Seedling from Mr. Carl Betscher; introduced by Fairmont Iris Gardens and strongly recommended by Mrs. Nesmith.

AMBER. Quoting from a letter from Mr. George Yeld received in 1930, "I have flowered one new plant this summer (the parentage is lost) which pleases me well. The color is somewhat between *flava* and *citrina*, the shape is good, the stature satisfactory. I am calling it Amber." Later Mr. Yeld wrote that he considers this "one of the best of the *Hemerocallis*." A halftone illustration of the flowers of Amber is shown in *New Flora and Silva* in 1931 (**3**: figure 71).

APRICOT (plate 12). Early flowering; semi-dwarf in stature, about 30 inches tall; compact in crown; foliage dark green; scapes erect, somewhat branched, usually slightly shorter than tallest of the leaves; the flowers are full, widely open, almost cadmium yellow in color and somewhat odorous. Apricot is a variety of charm and beauty and is distinct from the other early-flowering sorts now in the trade.

The Apricot Daylily is, apparently, the first hybrid daylily of which there is a definite record. It was exhibited in London in June 1892 as a seedling reared by Mr. George Yeld and it was awarded a Certificate of Merit (*Gard. Chr.* **73**: 394. 1893). It was then considered to be a hybrid of "*H. flava* crossed with

H. fulva or *H. Middendorffii*," but Mr. Yeld is quoted with the statement that he had lost the details of the crosses. It is stated that Mr. Yeld had been working with *Hemerocallis* for some time and that he had "a good many seedlings."

Mr. George Yeld states (*Rep. Third Int. Conf. Genetics* p. 415) that *H. Middendorffii* and *H. flava* were the parents of Apricot. But Apricot does not closely resemble the hybrids which the writer has from this cross. My seedlings are more robust, the foliage remains green later in autumn, and the leaves are not pink at the base as in Apricot.

The Royal Horticultural Society reports (*Jour. Roy. Hort. Soc.* **57**: 108. 1932) that there are four different clones growing in their trial grounds which were received as Apricot. One of these was given the Award of Merit.

AURANTIACA MAJOR (see plate 8). The "*H. aurantiaca* var. *major*" described and illustrated in a drawing by Baker in 1895 (*Gard. Chr.* Ser. III: **18**: 62) was imported from Japan by Messrs. Wallace and Son. Flowers of it were exhibited before the Royal Horticultural Society in July of that year and received the First Class Certificate (*Proc. Roy. Hort. Soc.* **19**: CIXVIII). This daylily is very similar to the *H. aurantiaca* in habits of growth and in season of flowering, but the foliage is a darker shade of green and the flowers are much larger, more full, more widely spreading, and uniformly orange without fulvous coloring. At New York and northward, this daylily frequently suffers from winter injury and does not thrive and bloom freely. Plants of this so-called variety that are identical and appear to belong to a single clone have been obtained at The New York Botanical Garden from various sources in Europe and from cultivated stock in Japan, and certain plants of this clone received from Japan under the name "*Hemerocallis aurea.*" It is recorded (*Gard.* **48**: 400–401. 1895) that this plant appeared in cultivation in Japan and was probably a chance seedling possibly of accidental hybridization.

A colored plate of the *H. aurantiaca* clone Major was published

Plate 12. Plant and flowers of Apricot Daylily

Plate 13. *Above,* Estmere Daylily. *Below,* Aureole Daylily

in 1895 (*Gard.* **48**: plate 1041); a half-tone reproduction appeared in 1896 (*Gard.* **50**: 17). The photograph of a flower of this daylily together with one of the *H. aurantiaca* here shown in plate 8 also appeared in The New Flora and Silva for April, 1933.

AURELIA. Seedling seen by the author at Mr. Yeld's garden in 1930; said to be hybrid of *H. aurantiaca* × *H. Middendorffii.* The open flower is clear orange-yellow with no fulvous markings.

AUREOLE (see plate 13). About 3 ft. tall; foliage rather coarse, evergreen; scapes coarse, erect-spreading, branching with conspicuous leafy bracts. Flowers numerous, full, wide-spreading, about 4 inches in diameter, not strongly reflexed, segments tapering, color rich cadmium yellow, with faint traces of brownish fulvous. The well-established plants of Aureole are very floriferous and the flowering climax is in June after the best early varieties are through blooming or waning, and for these reasons it is especially to be recommended. Received A. M. (Award of Merit) of Roy. Hort. Soc. in 1931.

Aureole is believed to be a hybrid from Japan; known as early as 1903 (*Gard.* **63**: 53); parentage has been assumed to be *H. Middendorffii* × *H. Dumortierii.* Stature, character of scapes and evergreen foliage, and a faint tinge of fulvous coloring in the flowers suggest *H. aurantiaca* as a parent.

AUSTIN, MRS. A. H. Distributed by Mr. Carl Betscher and Bay State Nurseries in 1929. Nearly 3 ft. tall. Flowers full, 4 in. diameter, well-shaped, clear orange. Blooms in late July.

BARDELEY. Mentioned in 1932 (*Hort.* **10**: 292) and listed by Mr. Amos Perry in his catalog of that autumn. Described as strong growing, with broad handsome foliage and stout stems bearing large open flowers of a distinct shade of orange-apricot, with a faint central red zone, and with distinct sulphur lines running through the inner petals.

BARONI. One of the first hybrids with *H. citrina* as a parent; produced by Mr. Willy Müller and his uncle Charles Sprenger;

described first in 1903 (*Gard. Chr.* **34**: 122). Baroni is night-blooming and otherwise similar to *H. citrina,* but has a fuller flower.

BAY STATE. Seedling from Mr. Carl Betscher; listed in 1929. Described as 4 ft. tall; large deep-yellow flowers; climax of bloom about July 20. Flowers similar to those of the Framingham Daylily.

BEAUTY. Hybrid of *H. flava* × *H. Dumortierii;* mentioned by Mr. Yeld in 1906 (*Rep. Third Conf. of Genetics* p. 417); "a shapely, round, well-opened flower with dark maroon back." In 1933, Mr. Yeld wrote to the writer as follows, "Beauty I believe is the same as Sovereign. I raised Beauty before Sovereign appeared but as the name Sovereign appeared first I withdrew the name Beauty."

BETSCHER, ANNA, or BETSCHER, A. Seedling from Mr. Carl Betscher; listed in 1929. Plants with stiff branched scapes, 3 ft. tall. Flowers large, 5 in. diameter, full, recurving, empire yellow. Plants are floriferous and they bloom through late July and early August. See plate 14.

BIJOU (see plate 15). The daylily is a selection from many seedlings of a new race of small-flowered daylilies developed at The New York Botanical Garden by hybridizations with the wild species *Hemerocallis multiflora.* It was first described with photographs showing flowers and habit of growth in the *Jour. N. Y. Bot. Garden* (**33**: 1–4).

The plant is vigorous in growth and there is a rapid but compact spread of branches in the crown. The foliage is abundant, rather erect-ascending, with the upper levels only slightly below the flowers. The scapes rise to a height of at least 2 ft. and stand slightly above the leaves; they are stiffly erect and much branched. The flowers are full, their segments spreading but not strongly reflexed, and they have a spread of about 2½ inches. The ground color is a shade of orange, showing clear in the throat of the flower but otherwise strongly overcast with rich fulvous red with darker mid-zone in a combination of sprightly color effects. The season of flowering is in July.

The seed parent of the Bijou Daylily is itself a complex hybrid having in its ancestry the species *H. aurantiaca*, *H. flava*, and *H. fulva* clone Europa. The plant of *H. multiflora* used as the pollen parent has tall, erect, and much-branched scapes, and it is somewhat earlier in blooming than the other plants of the species. Thus the Bijou Daylily is a hybrid with four distinct species involved in its parentage. As to flower color it is classed as fulvous; in flower size it is very similar to the *H. multiflora*, but the flowers are of a different shape. In its general ensemble of characteristics the Bijou Daylily is a somewhat distinct and new type among the horticultural daylilies.

BOWLES, E. A. Mentioned in 1926 (*Gard. Chr.* **80**: 126) with a halftone reproduction of a flower. Received from Mr. Perry in 1931. Tall, to 50 inches, with scapes well above leaves. Flowers, with petals rather narrow, pale fulvous, without eye zone, the color of the throat extending in a median stripe into the segments. This is a fulvous daylily; very similar to numerous seedlings grown by the writer from wild parentage.

BURBANK. Mentioned by Mr. B. Y. Morrison in 1924 (*Cir. 42*). Evidently produced by Luther Burbank and first listed by Mr. Carl Purdy. Plants obtained from Mr. Purdy are as much as 34 inches tall and the flowers are yellow with rather narrow segments. Very like *H. Thunbergii*.

BUTTERCUP. Mentioned in 1908 (*Rev. Hort.* **80**: 94) as being amply and widely open, odorous, and yellow like fresh butter.

BYNG OF VIMY. Seedling from Mr. Perry. Described in 1931 (*Gard. Chr.* **90**: 151) as "A distinct *Hemerocallis* with exceptionally large flowers, fully 5½ inches across, having long, loose perianth segments, in color dark terracotta bronze, overlaid with orange and deep orange at the base; the height is 4 ft."

CALYPSO (plate 16). Listed as early as 1929 by Mr. Carl Purdy, and origin credited to Luther Burbank. Plant with dark green rather erect foliage; numerous branched scapes, stiffly erect to a height of about 3 ft. Blooms during July. The flowers are numerous, full, rather large, clear lemon-yellow. Calypso is night-blooming and the flowers remain open during the hours of daylight only when the weather is cool.

CHARMAINE. A seedling of wild stock developed at The New York Botanical Garden by selective breeding in the *H. fulva* variety *rosea*. The flower is a clear rosy-pink of a shade that closely approaches pink. One of the best of the seedlings thus far obtained in this type. The period of flowering is in July.

CHOCOLATE SOLDIER. See GIUSEPPE, CISSY.

CHRISTII. Mention in 1908 (*Rev. Hort.* **80**: 94) states that the flowers are large and yellow-orange. Later (*Rev. Hort.* **80**: 99) it is said to be identical to Parthenope. Apparently now not in culture.

CHROME–ORANGE. A seedling raised by Mr. Theodore L. Mead of Oviedo, Florida, and to some extent distributed by him. Described in a letter received by the writer during 1933 as similar to Florham but with flowers deeper orange. The segments of the flowers are more narrow than in Florham.

CHRYSOLITE. Hybrid by Mr. Yeld of *H. Thunbergii* × *H. aurantiaca*; mentioned in 1906 *(Rep. Third Conf. Genetics)*; described as having large pale-yellow flowers.

CHRYSOLORA. Mentioned in a letter from Mr. Amos Perry in 1925. Described in 1932 (*Jour. Roy. Hort. Soc.* **57**: 111); "Foliage 2½ feet tall, spreading, medium green. Flower stems widely branched near the summit, 10- to 20-flowered; bracts conspicuous. Flowers 4½ inches in diameter, somewhat star-like, sulphur-apricot, deeper in the throat. Flowering from July 3 to August 5."

CINNABAR (plate 8). The special charm of this daylily is in the rich fulvous coloring of its flowers. The throat of the

Plate 14. *Above*, Anna Betscher Daylily. *Below*, Golden Dream Daylily

Plate 15. Flowers of the Bijou Daylily

Plate 16. The night-blooming Calypso Daylily

flower is a clear cadmium yellow; the outer half of the petals is covered or at times somewhat streaked with a vinacious-rufous shade of red and the sepals are somewhat more solidly of this color. The flowers are, therefore, of a rich but delicate shade of brownish red and they have good size, are widely open, and numerous. The plant has an excellent and semi-robust habit of growth. At New York, Cinnabar blooms in July.

The Cinnabar Daylily is one of about 150 seedlings obtained by crossing the garden clone Luteola with *H. aurantiaca.* Of the numerous seedlings obtained which have fulvous coloring, Cinnabar was judged to be the best. Its fulvous coloring is more intensified than that of the *H. aurantiaca.*

Cinnabar was offered to the trade by the Farr Nursery Co., in 1930, and it was described and the flowers illustrated in 1931 (*Jour. N. Y. Bot. Garden* **32**: 27–28).

CITRONELLA. A hybrid of *H. citrina* and probably *H. Thunbergii,* reared by Mr. Betrand Farr; introduced in 1926. It has an excellent foliage, is floriferous, and the pale yellow flowers are fuller than those of *H. citrina,* but they are night-blooming. Has been discontinued by the Farr Nursery Company.

CORONA. One of the first hybrids obtained by Mr. George Yeld from *H. flava* × *H. aurantiaca* clone Major; first reported in 1905 (*Gard. Chr.* **68**: 28); described as having large and stately flowers, richly orange-colored, and fragrant. Said to be very similar to Queen of May (*Jour. Roy. Hort. Soc.* **57**: 108. 1932).

CRAWFORD, J. A. A seedling from Mr. Betscher; offered to the trade in 1929. The flowers are of good size, apricot and cadmium yellow, and borne on stems about 4 feet tall; blooms in late June continuing into July. The flowers are very similar to those of the Mrs. J. R. Mann and the Mrs. W. H. Wyman Daylilies.

CRESSIDA. Seedling from Mr. Betscher; offered to the trade in 1929 by Bay State Nurseries. About 3 ft. tall; flowers reach

5 inches in spread, full, spreading, rich orange in color with tinge of fulvous. Blooms in July.

CROWN OF GOLD. Listed in 1933 catalog of Fairmont Iris Gardens and described as "a very clear deep orange flower of great beauty; large open flowers on tall stems, making a brilliant garden subject; three feet; May–June."

CURIOSITY. Described in 1931 (*Gard. Chr.* **90**: 151) as rich rosy-buff, pale sulphur sepals, conspicuously tipped with crimson with a sulphur-yellow base.

CYGNET. Mentioned by Mr. Morrison in 1924 (*House Beautiful* **55**: 69) and origin credited to Luther Burbank.

DAWN. Listed by Mr. Perry in his autumn catalog of 1932; described as "large bell-formed flowers nearly 5 inches across, pretty shade of rose-buff, sulphur petals, conspicuously tipped crimson, sulphur base."

DEAN, WILLIAM. Reported by Mr. George Yeld in 1906 (*Rep. Third Int. Conf. Genetics*, p. 415) as a sister hybrid to Flame, Estmere, and Beauty, and as somewhat similar to Gold Dust, Sovereign, and Orangeman. The parents said to be *H. flava* and *H. Dumortierii.* Described "as tall as flava, is of deeper orange with little maroon on the back of the flower." Not in the trade now.

DWARF YELLOW. Obtained from the Bristol Nurseries in 1930. Not dwarf. Scapes to 32 inches, coarse, ascending. Flower large (to a width of 5½ inches) widely open, clear yellow-orange. Blooms in late June.

ELDORADO. Plant to 42 inches; foliage dark green, pink-tinged at the base, rather robust and ascending, but not coarse. Flower about 5 inches in spread, segments spreading, somewhat wavy, light cadmium in color. Blooms in July. Seedling of Mr. Perry; about 1926.

ELEMENSE. Mentioned in 1903 (*Gard Chr.* **34**: 122) as a hybrid of *H. minor* × *H. citrina;* reared by Willy Müller and Charles Sprenger. The writer is informed by Mr. Müller that the seedling named Elemense was from the cross *H. minor* × *H. Thunbergii* and that the plant has been lost to culture, at least at Hortus Nucerensis.

ERICA. Mentioned in a letter from Mr. Amos Perry about in 1925. The plants which the author has obtained from Mr. Perry under this name appear to be identical with the clone of *H. aurantiaca* described in page 31.

ESTMERE (see plate 13). In habit of growth the Estmere Daylily somewhat resembles *H. Dumortierii* but it is more robust, the scapes are branched, and the flowers are more numerous. Also the flowers are medium full, widely spreading, and pale yellowish orange. The somewhat slender scapes spread and bend gracefully from the crown bringing the flowers into various levels with the greater number in the outer rim of the dome of foliage.

Estmere is one of the early hybrids produced by Mr. George Yeld and reported by him in 1906 (*Rep. Third Conf. Genetics*, p. 415–417).

EUROPA. *Hemerocallis fulva* clone Europa, see page 23.

FLAME. An early hybrid of Mr. Yeld's; mentioned by him as better than *H. Dumortierii* and more striking in color (*Gard. Chr.* **85**: 123. 1929). Said to be (*Rep. Third Conf. Genetics*, p. 415. 1906) of *H. flava* × *H. Dumortierii* and described as "orange with maroon on the back of the flower, and having deep maroon buds, and not as tall as *H. flava*.

FLAMID. This clone is very similar to Sovereign and Gold Dust in habit of growth, and in size, shape and disposition of flowers. The flower color is almost as in Gold Dust.

FLAMMEA. Mentioned in 1906 (*Gard. Chr.* **39**: 409) as "a new early flowering variety of rich yellow color." May be same as Flamid.

FLAVA MAJOR. Mentioned in 1908 (*Rev. Hort.* **80**: 94) as a variety of *H. flava* but taller. Plants of this name, obtained from Farr Nursery Co., in 1925, are of two different clones.

Compared with *H. flava,* they are taller, later in season of blooming, with flowers paler and less full. Two types are mentioned (*Jour. Roy. Hort. Soc.* **57**: 107); one identical with *H. flava,* and one similar but with darker foliage and with the apex of the petals more reflexed and the margin wavy. Two somewhat different clones have also been received under the name "*H. flava Major*" at The New York Botanical Garden. Evidently these are hybrid seedlings rather than a true variety of the species *H. flava.*

FLAVO-CITRINA. This name was given by H. Christ in 1898 (*Abhandl. Natur. Verein Bremen* **14**: 273) to a spontaneous garden hybrid supposed to be of *H. flava* and *H. Middendorffii.* But the descriptions make it certain that the plant called *H. Middendorffii* was *H. Dumortierii.* A good colored plate of the hybrid is published, evidently the first for any hybrid daylily, which shows a much-branched scape and a dark brownish-red coloring of sepals and tube. Evidently this hybrid was somewhat like Sovereign. The use of the "*citrina*" in this name has no reference to the *H. citrina* named and described later in the same year.

FLORHAM. In 1899 the following statement was published (*The Florists Exchange* **11**: 170). "A. Herrington, Madison, N. Y., registers a new *Hemerocallis* 'Florham'; *H. aurantiaca major* + *H. Thunbergii.* Habit of plant intermediate between parents. The foliage has the distichous arrangement of *H. aurantiaca major,* but the leaves are narrower, more elongated, and arching outward after the manner of *H. Thunbergii.* Flower spikes erect, three to four feet in height, bearing five to six branches each producing six to seven flowers. Flowers, when expanded are about six inches in diameter; sepals four inches long, three-quarters of an inch broad, yellow, suffused orange, some flowers showing well-defined bands of this hue through the entire length of sepal. Petals four inches long, one and one-quarter inches broad and of a clear canary-yellow color."

In a letter to the author, written during 1929, Mr. Arthur Herrington states that *H. Thunbergii* and "*H. aurantiaca major*" were crossed "both ways and a batch of seedlings resulted therefrom. The first ones that flowered were named Florham but as others developed they showed considerable variation. No attempt was made to exploit or introduce the plant so it drifted into cultivation by pieces given away. In all its variant types, however, it was free-flowering and tall growing."

The New York Botanical Garden has received three clones under the name Florham that are noticeably different in various minor characteristics. Several seedlings either of this particular group of hybrids or of other hybrids are being distributed under the name Florham.

FRAMINGHAM. Seedling from Mr. Betscher. Distributed about 1930 by Bristol Nurseries. Blooms in July; height about 3 feet, flowers rich orange, full, and of good size.

FRANCIS. Received the Award of Merit from the Royal Horticultural Society in 1895. Mr. Yeld states it was a hybrid between *H. minor* and *H. Middendorffii* (*Gard. Chr.* **85**: 123. 1929) and that it was like Apricot but more dwarf (*Rep. Third Cong. Genetics* p. 415. 1906). This clone seems to have disappeared from culture.

FULCITRINA. This name was given by Mr. Willy Müller to certain hybrids between the Maculata Daylily and *H. citrina*. These were listed for the trade as early as 1908, but may have been distributed earlier; some of them may still be in existence. The F_1 generation of this cross which the writer has seen are all night-blooming, pale fulvous, and the flowers have rather narrow petals; and are of no merit as garden plants. Mention of a plant of "Ful-citrina" is made in 1907 (*Gard. Chr.* **42**: 188) as "dull and worthless." The same is true of similar hybrids between certain types of *H. fulva* and *H. citrina* or "*H. graminea*" (*H. minor*) reared at the University of Strasbourg some time prior to 1908 (*Gartenflora* **57**: 362), some of which the writer has obtained through the kindness of Professor Charles Killian.

FULVA–CYPRIANA. In 1903, Charles Sprenger reported seed and seedlings of various types of *H. fulva.* Evidently the *H. fulva* clone Cypriana was used as a pollen parent with some other fulvous daylily, for a seedling with some such parentage found its way into culture in England. Mention is made that it came from Charles Sprenger and the description (*Gard. Chr.* **42**: 188. 1907) is as follows, "A most distinct and beautiful variety, with regularly formed flowers that expand well. In color they are a clear brown shade, with a clearly defined and slightly raised yellow midrib down the center of each of the alternate petals. This is one of the most beautiful *Hemerocallis* known to me." At the time this was written, there were few clones of fulvous daylilies in culture in England. This description of the coloring applies fairly well to various wild plants and to numerous seedlings which the writer has grown but which are not considered of sufficient merit for distribution.

FULVAX. Listed in the catalog for 1931 of the Fairmont Iris Gardens and described as similar in coloring to the Europa Daylily but better. No information as to the origin seems available and the writer has not seen this plant in flower.

GAY DAY. Seedling from Mrs. Thomas Nesmith, listed in the catalog of Fairmont Iris Gardens for 1933 and described as "well-formed soft-yellow flowers with great substance and beauty, borne on sturdy stems of good height. The last to bloom in my garden; Aug.–Sept.; 3 feet."

GAYNER, J. S. A seedling from Mr. Yeld described in 1928 (*Gard. Illus.* Aug. 11, p. 510) as "The large deep yellow flowers of this variety are more widely expanded than those of most daylilies." Received Award of Merit from Royal Horticultural Society in 1931. Described in 1932 (*Jour. Roy. Hort. Soc.* **57**: 111); "Very vigorous, forming dense tufts of medium green foliage, 3 feet in height. Flower stands 40 inches tall, erect, well branched at the apex 8- to 14-flowered. Flowers 4½ inches diameter, wide, open funnel-shaped, soft orange-apricot, scented; petals broad, thick, tips reflexed, margins wavy. Seeding sparsely in ovate capsules. Flowering very freely from July 1 to August 20."

GEM, THE. Listed by Mr. Carl Betscher and by Bay State Nurseries in 1929. Robust; scapes to 38 inches, medium coarse, branched, well above leaves. Flowering in July. Flowers full, slightly over 4 inches in spread, color light cadmium. Very similar to Miranda, but flower color slightly more orange. Similar to Luteola but more robust.

GIUSEPPE, CISSY. Seedling from Mr. Amos Perry. At first called Chocolate Soldier. First mentioned in 1931 (*Gard. Chr.* **90**: 151) and listed by Mr. Perry in autumn catalog of 1932. Described as having stout rigid stems 2½ feet tall, and medium-sized flowers deep rosy-bronze with yellow base. Flowering in midsummer.

GLOBE D'OR. Mentioned by Mr. B. Y. Morrison (*Cir.* 42).

GOLCONDA. Hybrid with *H. citrina* as one parent; produced by Mr. Farr in 1824. Height 40 inches; flowers large, segments rather narrow, light cadmium in color, night-blooming. Discarded by the Farr Nursery Company.

GOLD BALL. Offered to the trade in 1910 by Willy Müller of Naples, Italy. He obtained the plant from the Botanical Garden of Strasbourg University. Said to be one of six varieties having *H. flava* and some type of *H. fulva* as parents. The others were listed as Professor Kirschlege, Professor Krause, Orange, Professor Jost, and Professor Stahl.

Mention of these hybrids was made in 1907 (*Gartenflora* **57**: 362) in the report of a display before Des Vereins zur Beförderung des Gartenbauses in den preussischen Staaten. It is stated that a Mr. Müller, head gardener at the University of Strasbourg had hybridized *H. graminea* and *H. citrina* with *H. fulva* as a mother plant. It is not known if the "*H. fulva*" referred to was the old *H. fulva* clone Europa or some of the newer wild types.

GOLD DUST (see plates 17 and 30). Illustrated in color in *Addisonia* **15**: plate 186. 1930. One of the best of the early flowering semi-dwarf daylilies having *H. Dumortierii* as one parent. There is a compact habit of growth; the foliage is light green, and rather erect to a height of about two feet. The scapes are stout, stiffly erect to a height of several inches above the leaves, rather freely short-branched, and bearing as many as ten flowers to a scape. The flower buds are tinged with dull red. The inner face of the open flower is a clear uniform shade of yellow very near to light cadmium. The flower is fairly full with petals about one inch in greatest width, and the expanded flower has a spread of about three inches. The flowers have a somewhat extended period of opening (plate 30).

Of the origin of this clone, Mr. George Yeld states in 1906 (*Rep. Third Conf. Genetics* page 415) that the Daylilies Gold Dust, Sovereign, and Orangeman were then already in the trade, and that these are "very similar to if not identical with" his own hybrids between the species *H. flava* and *H. Dumortierii* which he had named Flame, Estmere, William Dean, and Beauty. In general all these plants are somewhat intermediate between the two supposed parents. Gold Dust unmistakably shows in its dull red flower buds and in other qualities that *H. Dumortierii* is one of the parents, but its scapes are stiffly erect and well-branched and it is a better garden plant, being more floriferous and having larger and fuller flowers. The upstanding scapes and foliage of Gold Dust, Sovereign, and Flamid are in decided contrast to the spreading foliage and scapes of Estmere and Orangeman.

GOLD IMPERIAL. Described in 1925 (*Gard. Chr.* **77**: 166) as "rich golden-orange, broad petals waved and crinkled, 2½ feet tall, blooms in July." The flowers are strongly night-blooming. Described in 1932 (*Jour. Roy. Hort. Soc.* **57**: 111) "Foliage medium green, 2½ feet tall. Flower stems 3 feet tall, erect, branched towards the top, 10- to 20-flowered. Flowers 4½ inches diameter, somewhat star-like, bright chrome-yellow,

Plate 17. Gold Dust Daylily and Tangerine Daylily

Plate 18. *Above*, Jubilee Daylily. *Below*, Princess Daylily

reverse darker, margins of petals wavy. Seeds freely in oval capsules. Flowering freely from July 3 to August 15."

GOLD STANDARD. A seedling reared by Mr. Amos Perry; listed for sale by him in 1925. Described as having "broad, full, deep canary-yellow flowers, scented, full-blooming, 2½ feet tall" (*Gard. Chr.* **78**: 166). Described in 1932 (*Jour. Roy. Hort. Soc.* **57**: 112) as "vigorous, forming close tufts of dark green foliage, 28 inches in height. Flower stems 38 inches tall, erect, widely branched above the middle, side branches tinged purple, 15- to 30-flowered. Flowers 4 inches diameter, wide funnel-shaped, opening lemon and quickly passing to soft apricot-chrome, reverse tinged brown at tips. Seeds freely. Flowering freely from July 13 to August 28."

GOLDEN BELL. Introduced by Messrs. Wallace of Colchester, England in 1915. Received the Award of Merit from Royal Horticultural Society that year (*Jour. Roy. Hort. Soc.* **41**: CXXVII) and the statement was made that it is "A handsome seedling of *H. flava* bearing large deep, lemon-yellow flowers with broad segments. Later that year an uncolored plate was published (*Gard.* **79**: 350–354) and note made that "The rich yellow flowers of this fine Daylily have somewhat of the form and properties of *H. aurantiaca major*."

In 1932 (*Jour. Roy. Hort. Soc.* **57**: 109), it is stated that this and Orangeman are similar in habit and foliage and the following description is given. "Vigorous; forming close clumps, with dark green arching foliage, 2 feet in height. Flower stems 2½ feet tall, branching above and below the middle very widely, 8- to 16-flowered. Flowers 4¾ inches diameter, flat funnel-shaped, soft apricot-orange, throat darker; petals broad; recurved at the tips, inner somewhat wavy; scented. Seeds sparingly. Flowering from June 24 to August 5." Rated as Highly Commended by the Royal Horticultural Society in 1931.

The two descriptions noted above do not agree, for the flowers of *H. aurantiaca* clone Major and those of Orangeman are very different.

The writer has plants received from the Farr Nursery Company under the name Golden Bell that have scapes about 3 feet tall and full flowers near empire yellow in color. This plant resembles Luteola but has somewhat larger flowers.

GOLDEN DREAM. Seedling from Mr. Betscher, cataloged by him in 1929. About 3 feet tall; flowers rich clear orange in color; rather full; bloom in late July. See plate 14.

GOLDEN DUST. Listed by Mr. Willy Müller in 1908. Probably same as Gold Dust.

GOLDEN WEST. Produced by Mr. H. P. Sass. Introduced by Fairmont Iris Gardens in 1932. A Hybrid of *H. citrina* and *H. aurantiaca* clone Major.

GOLDENI. Seedling reared by Mr. Betscher and offered to trade in 1929; described as 3 feet tall, with deep golden orange flowers, vigorous in habit, and a most effective garden variety. An uncolored illustration of the flower appeared in 1931 (*Hort.* 9: 367).

GRACILIS. Offered in the trade under this name are several early-flowering clones usually about 2 feet tall with narrow leaves and flowers of yellow or light orange colors. The name is often given as for a species (*H. gracilis*). The origin and the status of these plants are somewhat uncertain, but some of them strongly resemble *H. minor*.

GRAMINEA CROCEA. Listed by Willy Müller as early as 1910; said to be very similar to the so-called *H. graminea*, which it seems should be called *H. minor*.

GYPSY. Seedling from Mr. Betscher, offered by the trade in 1929. Plant to 4½ feet; scapes and foliage are coarse. Flowers are light orange, full but not extra large (spread about 4 inches). Flowers in late July.

HALO. Reported by Mr. George Yeld (*Rep. Third Conf. Genetics.* 1906) as a hybrid of *H. Thunbergii* × *H. aurantiaca* and described as having a round flower with broad petals and a halo around the center of the inside of the flower.

HARVEST MOON. About 3 feet tall; flowers light orange, segments rather narrow. Seedling from Mr. Betscher, offered by Bay State Nurseries in 1929.

HIPPEASTROIDES. A hybrid produced by Willy Müller and Charles Sprenger; mentioned 1908 (*Gard. Chr.* **54**: 122). According to Mr. Müller it has been lost to culture at Hortus Nucerensis. May be the same as Hippeastrum. Mr. Müller states to the writer that the parentage was "*H. minor crocea* × *H. Thunbergii.*"

HIPPEASTRUM. Briefly mentioned in 1925 (*Gard. Chr.* **77**: 247). Resembles *H. Thunbergii* in habit and flower color, but blooms earlier. Flower buds clustered and often in whirls, tinged with reddish brown. Flowers have narrow sepals that tend to stand erect after petals are reflexed.

HOLMES, MRS. CARL. Briefly mentioned in 1931 (*Gard. Chr.* **90**: 151) as having flowers 4½ inches across.

HUME, EMILY. Seedling of unknown origin, observed by H. Harold Hume among a number of plants of the clone Florham. Named by Mr. Hume in 1933 and the following description was supplied by him.

"The plants form good masses, 18 to 24 inches in height; evergreen; leaves to 37 inches, ¾ inches wide, channeled, dark green, somewhat glaucous. Scapes slender, to 36 inches, branching, compact, bearing 6 to 12 flowers. Flowers large, 4½ to 5 inches across the normally expanded petals, opening moderately wide; color medium yellow (dandelion, Maerz and Paul; 9 L-4), glistening, the three sepals reflexed, tinted green at the base, rather spatulate, the apex rounded, terminated in a small short tip or point; striated on the outer surface, with a shallow channel paralleling the slightly crimped margins. The three petals are larger, "pinched"[1] a short distance back of the apex.

[1] The word "pinched" is used to describe the folding back of the petals. They appear as though somebody had taken them between their fingers and bent them back in such manner that they remained in place.

Margins of the five upper parts of the perianth touching, the lowest one separated from the ones on each side. In full bloom in northern Florida during the first week in May. The "pinched" flowers resemble those of Wau-Bun in shape, but differ in color and in the spacing of the petals.

HYPERION. A seedling reared by Franklin B. Mead; listed for sale in 1925. Reported to be Sir Michael Foster × Florham. The stout rigid stems arise to a level of 40 inches; the flowers are 5 to 6 inches in spread, full, numerous, odorous, and the color is a canary-yellow of a shade paler than the Lemon Daylily. Blooms through late July. A half-tone illustration of the flower appeared in 1924 (Gard. **88**: 703). Received Award of Merit of Royal Horticultural Society in 1931.

IMPERATOR. A seedling from Mr. Perry; noted in 1931 (*Gard. Chr.* **90**: 151) as having "large, open, star-shaped flowers, 5 inches across, with sharp-pointed perianth segments, rich orange-red, lined with sulphur, and rich orange at the base." This plant has flowers with narrow petals and color rather characteristic of various plants of the wild type of *H. fulva.*

JOST, PROFESSOR. See the discussion of Gold Ball.

JUBILEE (plate 18). This daylily is similar to Mikado in habit of growth and in the size and shape of the conspicuously eyed flowers; but the flower, except for the zone of English red in the petals, is light cadmium or almost yellow. The scapes are much branched and reach a height of about 3½ feet. The period of flowering at New York is in July. In obtaining Jubilee a seedling of *H. aurantiaca* × *H. fulva* wild from China was crossed with Mikado.

KESTON. Mention of a daylily with this name was made by Mr. Amos Perry in a letter written in 1929. Three plants received from Mr. Perry under this name are double-flowered with fulvous coloring and are apparently the same as certain of the older types known as Kwanso or Flore-Pleno.

KIRSCHLEGE, PROFESSOR. See discussion of Gold Ball.

KRAUSE, PROFESSOR. See Gold Ball.

LADHAMS, B. Plant at least 3 feet tall; flower clear yellow orange, rather full, spreading to width of about 4 inches, larger and slightly darker orange than Luteola. Blooms at New York in July. Described (*Jour. Roy. Hort. Soc.* **57**: 108. 1932) as follows:—"Much resembles Semperflorens except that the flower stems are less branched, the flowers smaller, paler and less freely borne. Flowering from June 22 to July 12."

LADY HESKETH or LADY FERMOY HESKETH. A hybrid from Mr. Amos Perry; *H. Thunbergii* × *H. citrina*. Displayed and received Award of Merit in 1924 (*Jour. Roy. Hort. Soc.* **50**: XCI). Scapes to 46 inches, erect, stiff, branched; flower almost 5 inches spread; pale yellow, segments narrow, often closed at 11:00 A.M. Illustrated in halftone (*Gard. Chr.* **65**: 123. 1929). Described in 1932 (*Jour. Roy. Hort. Soc.* **57**: 112); "Habit of 'Ochroleuca' except that the foliage is tinged with grey. Flowers 4 inches diameter, a shade darker than 'Ochroleuca' with broader petals, the reverse darker. Seeds freely born in short oval capsules. Flowering very freely from July 8 to August 22."

LATEST. See Mrs. W. H. Wyman.

LEMON KING. Listed by Fairmont Iris Gardens in autumn of 1932. Said to be a seedling from Mr. Carl Betscher.

LEMON QUEEN. Introduced by Bertrand Farr in 1926. Somewhat similar to Ophir but night-blooming. Discontinued by the Farr Nursery Company.

LEMONA. A seedling from Mr. Betscher. Distributed in 1928 by Mr. Betscher, The Bay State Nurseries, and The Bristol Nurseries. As tall as 5 feet; flowers pale lemon yellow, large (4½ inches in spread), numerous, somewhat night-blooming, and often closed at 11:00 A.M. on warm sunny days, at least when exposed to the sunlight.

LOVETT'S LEMON. Introduced by Lovett's Nursery. Pale yellow flower, rather narrow petals, not good day-blooming.

LOVETT'S ORANGE. Introduced by Lovett's Nursery. Concerning this daylily and the Lovett's Lemon, Mr. C. V. Lovett states in 1931 in a letter to the writer as follows: "The two *Hemerocallis* mentioned in your letter (Lovett's Orange and Lovett's Lemon) were both originations of the late Dr. W. Van Fleet. We regret that we have no record of the date when these two *Hemerocallis* were introduced, but, unless we are in error, they were originated between fifteen and eighteen years ago."

Plants of this clone are about 4 feet tall; flowers yellow rather than orange, with narrow petals and long slender tube, fading and closing on sunny days.

LUTEOLA. Illustrated in color in *Addisonia* **15**: plate 485. 1930. That the Luteola Daylily is a hybrid of horticultural origin is certain, but there is some discrepancy in the published statements regarding its parentage. What appears to be the first reference to it (*Gard.* **57**: 407. 1900) calls it a hybrid between "*H. aurantiaca major*" and *H. Thunbergii* but does not report the place of origin. In 1903 this same journal credits Messrs. R. Wallace and Co., of England with the hybridization, but states that the same cross was also made by a continental firm. In the summer of 1905 an Award of Merit was voted by the Royal Horticultural Society to a daylily which was exhibited by Messrs. R. Wallace and Co. under the name "*Hemerocallis* × *luteola*," and the parentage is recorded as being *H. aurantiaca* × *H. Thunbergii*. A plant of "*H. luteola*" is also credited to the hybridizer Sedon (*Gard. Chr.* 3rd Ser. **36**: 465) as a seedling of the cross between *H. aurantiaca* and "*H. aurantiaca major*." The custom of giving a single name of scientific and botanic rank, as was evidently done in this case, to various seedlings of hybrid origin which differ somewhat from each other and which are later propagated as horticultural clones leads only to confusion.

Several somewhat different clones have been received at The New York Botanical Garden under the name Luteola, the differences being in the size of the plants and in the shade of yellow of flowers and in their fullness. The clone, believed to be derived from the seedling reared by Messrs. R. Wallace and Co., has a plant of compact growth, with foliage that reaches a level of about 28 inches, and scapes that are about 3 feet tall and branched above. The flowers are full, well-expanded to a width of about 5 inches, of a color slightly darker than lemon chrome, and the perianth tube is stout and greenish in color. At New York the period of blooming begins about the middle of June.

LUTEOLA GRANDIFLORA. Mentioned in 1928 (*Cir. 42*) as "somewhat finer than the others" of the Luteola group. Mentioned in 1932 (*Jour. Roy. Hort. Soc.* **57**: 112) as very similar to "Luteola major" except that the flowers are larger with wavy margins. The names "grandiflora, major, and pallens" were applied to seedlings evidently as if each represented a true variety.

This daylily was briefly mentioned in 1908 (*Rev. Hort.* **80**: 94) and a year later a colored illustration of the flower appeared (*Rev. Hort.* **81**: 60) with the statement that the plant was a seedling of "*H. aurantiaca major* × *H. Thunbergii*" reared by Lemoine. The illustration shows a flower of rich orange color.

LUTEOLA MAJOR. In 1932 Luteola Major was described (*Jour. Roy. Hort. Soc.* **57**: 112) as "very similar to Luteola except that the flower stems are dwarfed and more widely branched; foliage broader and flowers larger." Plants of Luteola Major received by The New York Botanical Garden from C. G. Van Tubergen of Haarlem, Holland have scapes much taller (to 48 inches) than those of Luteola and the flowers are fuller and larger. Possibly there is more than one clone of this name.

LUTEOLA PALLENS. Mentioned in 1907 (*Gard. Chr.* **42**: 188) as from Lemoine, France; listed by this firm as a hybrid of *H. Luteola* × *H. citrina*. A colored plate (*Rev. Hort.*

81: 60. 1909) shows a medium full flower about 5 inches in spread, of a pale yellow color; the statement is made that the plant is from *H. citrina* × *H. Thunbergii.* Taller than Luteola, flower less full, paler in color which is near lemon-yellow.

MAJESTIC (plate 19). A sister seedling of Taruga obtained by crossing Yellow Hammer with Wau-Bun. Here described for the first time. The plant is of vigorous growth with scapes almost 3 feet tall which hold the flowers slightly above the foliage. The flowers are full and large, with a spread of at least six inches, the petals are spreading-recurving and have slightly undulate margins. The color is a clear and uniform shade of orange. The period for flowering is in early July.

MANDARIN. Hybrid introduced by Mr. Farr in 1924. Robust, dark green foliage; scapes stiffly erect to 4½ feet, flowers yellow, petals narrow, flowers in July, night-blooming.

MANN, MRS. JAMES R. Obtained in 1930 from John Lewis Childs, Inc. of Flowerfield, Long Island, New York, who state in a letter to the writer that "We have no idea where this originated." Mrs. Thomas Nesmith (*Hort.* **10**: 292. 1932.) mentions a clone "J. R. Mann" as well as a "Mrs. J. R. Mann" Daylily, but it seems very probable that these are of the same clone. Nearly 4 feet tall; blooms in July; flowers slightly larger and more orange than Luteola, nearly same as Mrs. W. H. Wyman, but slightly smaller.

MARIGOLD. Seedling from Mr. Yeld. Received Award of Merit in 1931, and described (*Jour. Roy. Hort. Soc.* **57**: 110) as "vigorous; forming dense clumps of dark green foliage, 28 inches tall. Flower stems 30 inches tall, branched near the top, 4- to 8-flowered. Flower 3 inches diameter, short funnel-shaped, bright deep rich orange self; petals broad, overlapping. No fruits. Flowering very freely from June 16 to July 6."

MAY QUEEN. Mentioned in 1924 (*Gard. Chr.* **75**: 187) as very early, pretty shade of orange, and 3½ feet tall.

Plate 19. Majestic Daylily

Plate 20. Mikado Daylily

Plate 21. Plant of Mikado Daylily

MEEHAN. Mentioned by Mr. Morrison (*Cir. 42*) as valuable in blooming between early and late types. Probably one of the Meehan Hybrids described as, "orange, large, fragrant" in the Thomas Meehan Sons Trade List for 1915.

MEG. Seedling of Mr. Yeld's in 1930; said to have a pale open flower.

MIDDENDORFFIANA. Mentioned as early as 1878 (*Gard* **14**: 305) as a species; described as dwarf but vigorous and distinct from the other species. Plants received under this name from C. G. Van Tubergen are nearly identical to the more robust plants of *H. Middendorffii.* Seedlings of the Middendorfiana are rather uniform in the character of the flowers but vary somewhat in vigor of growth. My judgment is that Middendorffiana is merely a clone of the species *H. Middendorffii.*

MIKADO. Developed by the writer at The New York Botanical Garden and first described in *House and Garden* for July, 1929. The colored plate here shown in plate 20 is reproduced from *Addisonia* (**15**: plate 487) and the plate 21 is from the *Journal New York Botanical Garden* (**32**: 29. fig. 2). The foliage is medium coarse, somewhat evergreen, and stands at a level of about 2 feet. The scapes are ascending to about 3 feet or slightly above this height and loosely branched above. The flowers are at least 5 inches in spread, fairly full, with segments widely spreading-recurving. In the middle of each petal there is a large blotch of dark and almost purplish red of the shade called mahogany red which is bisected by a stripe of the same color as the blade. In the open flower these blotches combine to form an undulating zone of conspicuous dark red which is in sharp contrast to the rich orange of the rest of the flower. The outstanding charm of this daylily is in the bold contrasts in the coloring of the flowers. There is also good size, form, and fullness of flower, and an excellent and almost robust habit of growth. The season of bloom is during July. This plant has in its ancestry the fulvous daylilies *H. aurantiaca* and the *H. fulva* clone *Europa*, and it was obtained after three generations of selective breeding.

MINIKEN. Mentioned in a letter from Mr. George Yeld in 1933 as "a pretty dwarf variety" obtained from the cross *H. nana* × *H. flava.*

MIRANDA. Described by Mr. Yeld in 1929 (*Gard. Chr.* **85**: 123) as the best of his seedlings of *H. aurantiaca* × *H. flava.* Two distinct clones have come to The New York Botanical Garden from England under this name. This variety is described in 1932 (*Jour. Roy. Hort. Soc.* **57**: 107) as follows; "plant vigorous, forming dense tufts, with medium yellowish-green, arching foliage, 30 inches tall. Flower stems erect 42 inches tall, very widely branched just above the middle, 9- to 24-flowered. Flowers 4½ inches diameter, funnel-shaped, soft apricot, reverse darker, falling, petals of medium width, wavy at the margins. Seeds very sparsely produced. Flowering from May 30 to August 5."

MODESTY. Seedling from Mr. Betscher, listed in 1929. About 3 feet tall; flowers about 4 inches in spread, full, pale lemon yellow; has flowered at New York as early as the first half of June.

MOIDORE. Mr. Yeld stated to the writer in the summer of 1930 that this is a hybrid of *H. flava* × *H. nana,* and that the flowers are rich orange.

MOONSHINE. Described in 1932 (*Gard. Chr.* **90**: 151) as having flowers of "medium size, very lily-like in form and a pretty shade of reddish-orange-apricot, with a faint cream zone in the center." Seedling reared by Mr. Perry.

MÜLLERI (MUELLERI). Noted in 1903 by Mr. Charles Sprenger (*Gard. Chr.* **34**: 122) as the best of the hybrids which he then had of *H. Thunbergii* × *H. citrina.* The flowers are described as very large, sweet-scented, and opening at 4 o'clock. Described in 1932 (*Jour. Roy. Hort. Soc.* **57**: 111); "Very vigorous, forming close tufts of erect dark green foliage, 3 feet in height. Flower stems 4 feet tall, much yet not widely branched near the top, 12- to 20-flowered. Flowers 4 inches diameter, starry, primrose scented; petals narrow, pointed. Flowering very freely."

MUTABLILIS. Listed by Mr. Willy Müller in 1908 as one of the seedlings reared by him at the Hortus Nucerensis.

NADA (see plate 27). This daylily is one of four seedlings obtained by the author from hybridizing a plant of *H. nana* as a seed parent with a hybrid which had dark red flowers and which had in its ancestry *H. flava, H. aurantiaca*, and the Europa Daylily. The seedling named Nada is now three years old. Its foliage and scapes bend so low that the plant stands scarcely a foot tall. The flowers are rather large (about 4½ inches in spread) and of rich Morocco red and claret brown colors, not only in the face of the flowers but also on the back of the petals. The period of bloom is in late June and early July. The Nada daylily was first described, with the illustration here reproduced in plate 27, in the *Journal of the New York Botanical Garden* for January, 1934.

NIGHTINGALE, WINNIE. Mentioned in a letter from Mr. Perry in the autumn of 1932 as having "large open flowers, brilliant orange in color."

NOCERENSIS. Obtained by The New York Botanical Garden from Amos Perry in 1930. The flowers are almost lemon yellow, odorous, large (a petal is about 4 inches long). The foliage is coarse and the scapes are about 4 feet tall. At New York flowering begins about June 15.

NUCERENSIS. Mentioned by Mr. Yeld (*Gard. Chr.* **85**: 122. 1929) as coming to him from R. Wallace and Co. Probably same as Nocerensis.

OCHROLEUCA. Described in 1903 by Charles Sprenger (*Gard. Chr.* **34**: 122) as a hybrid of *H. Thunbergii* × *H. citrina*. Has good habit of growth, dark green and rather erect foliage, flowers are sweet-scented and sulphur-yellow. Sprenger states that the flowers open at 6 o'clock in the evening and remain so during the following day. At New York, on warm sunny days the flowers are usually closed before midday.

OMPHALE. Mentioned in a letter from Mr. George Yeld as "very strong, pale orange."

OPHIR (see plate 28). One of the best hybrids of *H. citrina* parentage. Reared by Bertrand Farr and introduced in 1924. Blooms in July; good day-blooming, floriferous, scapes rise 50 inches, and about 15 inches above level of foliage. Flower large, long trumpet-shaped, full, spreading, clear orange-yellow. Received Award of Merit from Royal Horticultural Society in 1931.

ORANGE. In 1910 Willy Müller of the Hortus Nucerensis in Naples, Italy offered a variety "Orange" which was one of six seedlings reared at the Botanical Garden of the University of Strasbourg. These were first said to be crosses of *H. flava* and *H. fulva.* Müller states that these were similar to the Fulcitrina hybrids but bloomed earlier (see Gold Ball). The plants of this name which the writer has obtained from C. G. Van Tubergen in 1925 are almost identical to those of Middendorffiana and *H. Middendorffii,* and are in no particular similar to the various hybrids which have fulvous daylilies as a parent.

ORANGE GEM. Obtained from Perry in 1925. Foliage at a level of about 15 inches and scapes about 34 inches tall, flowers are conspicuously well above foliage. Flower somewhat resembles that of *H. Middendorffii* but is larger: the color is a uniform light orange (cadmium yellow).

ORANGE GLOW. Described in 1927 (*Gard. Chr.* **82**: 66) as having "rich orange, broad-petaled flowers, produced very freely." Described in 1932 (*Jour. Roy. Hort. Soc.* **57**: 109) as "Habit similar to 'Taplow Orange' except that the flower stems are more widely branched with 9- to 16-flowers. Flowers 4 inches diameter, short funnel-shaped, bright orange-apricot. Seeding freely in long oval capsules. Flowering from June 12 to July 15."

ORANGE VASE. Described in 1932 (*Jour. Roy. Hort. Soc.* **57**: 109). "Habit of 'Taplow Orange' with darker foliage. Flower stems semi-erect, just topping the foliage, 3 feet tall, often twisted, 6- to 8-flowered. Flowers 3½ inches diameter, cup-shaped, bright rich orange-apricot. Flowers from June 16 to July 13."

ORANGEMAN. Very similar to Estmere in stature and habit of growth and disposition of branches but the flowers are more orange in color. The buds are somewhat dull red as in *H. Dumortierii*. Orangeman grows compactly and lustily and produces many flower stalks and numerous flowers. A well-grown plant in the author's garden had over 500 flowers during one season of bloom and on the day of climax flowering there were about 90 flowers open at one time. Mr. Yeld states (*Rep. Third Conf. Genetics*, p. 415) that Orangeman was already in the trade in 1906. Of its origin there seems to be no record. Orangeman, Estmere, Gold Dust, Sovereign, Apricot, and Tangerine all bloom during late May and early June.

PARTHENOPE. Hybrid said to be of "*H. Thunbergii* × *H. aurantiaca major*"; reported and described by Charles Sprenger in 1903 (*Gard. Chr.* **34**: 122). The writer has plants of Parthenope from Mr. Willy Müller of Naples, who made the hybridization and who has continued in the nursery business in Naples. The foliage is robust and dark green; the scapes rise to a height of 48 inches. The flower is funnel-shaped, rather large, but with rather narrow petals, odorous, and lemon-yellow in color. The plant blooms early in July and flowers are usually well open during the day. The base of the foliage is pinkish. This clone resembles Nocerensis and Sir Michael Foster and appears to have *H. citrina* in the parentage.

PERRY, AMOS. Described in 1905 (*Gard. Chr.* **38**: 204) as somewhat different from *H. citrina* in having flowers with shorter and broader petals.

PERRY, GLADYS. Described in 1931 (*Gard. Chr.* **90**: 151) as follows; "A new and distinct color is seen. Flowers are medium size, with broad over-lapping perianth segments, and the color is a telling shade of rosy-bronze, heavily lined with crimson and orange."

PERRY, IRIS. Listed by Mr. Perry in 1925 as a hybrid of *H. Thunbergii* × *H. aurantiaca.* Mentioned in 1931 (*Gard Chr.* **90**: 151) as having bold gracefully arching foliage and rich orange flowers. This daylily is almost identical to the *H. aurantiaca.*

PERRY, MARCUS. Mentioned in 1932 in a letter from Mr. Amos Perry as "distinct; pointed, tinted petals; orange flushed with brown."

PERRY, MARGARET (plate 7). Mentioned in 1925 under name of Maggie Perry (*Gard. Chr.* **77**: 166) as a hybrid of "*H. fulva* × *H. cypriana.*" The foliage is coarse, pale green, and rather robust. The scapes rise to as much as 54 inches. The flowers have medium narrow and pointed segments; the color in the throat is cadmium yellow with a stripe of this color extending out through the center of each segment; otherwise the segments are orange. Received the Award of Merit from Royal Horticultural Society in July, 1926, under the name of Maggie Perry. Illustrated in halftone (*Gard. Chr.* **85**: 59).

The plant is very similar to certain wild plants of *H. fulva* which the writer has received from China. These and the Margaret Perry often continue in bloom at New York from the middle of July until late in August.

PERRY, MRS. Listed by Mr. Amos Perry in 1925 as a hybrid of *H. Thunbergii* × *H. citrina.* Described in 1926 (*Gard. Chr.* **80**: 126) as "amaryllis-like, well-expanded flowers with short tubes. Delightful shade of rich old gold on stout well branched scapes fully 40 inches tall, sweet-scented." Described in 1932 (*Jour. Roy. Hort. Soc.* **57**: 111); "Foliage 2 feet tall, medium green, drooping at the tips. Flower stems 3 to 3½ feet tall, very close, branched at the apex, 8- to 14-flowered; bracts conspicuous. Flowers 5½ inches diameter, wide funnel-shaped apricot-orange, reverse darker, petals reflexed at tips, margins wavy. Seeds sparingly in wide oval capsules. Flowering from July 3 to August 2."

PERRY, REGGIE. Described in 1931 (*Gard. Chr.* **90**: 151) as "flowers remarkably handsome and of good form with bold overlapping petals, rich orange-yellow in color, and they are borne on tall well-branched stems, with an amaryllis-like appearance."

PERRY, THELMA. Mentioned in 1925 in letter from Mr. Amos Perry as seedling of *H. Thunbergii* × *H. citrina.* Described in 1926 (*Gard. Chr.* **80**: 126) with halftone illustration as "erect foliage, tall well-branched spikes, 3½ feet tall, each 15 to 20 flowers, blooming from July to September." At The New York Botanical Garden, this clonal variety is night-blooming with the flowers closing as early as 9:00 A.M. on warm sunny days.

PERRY'S PIGMY. Mentioned in 1932 in a letter from Mr. Perry as hybrid of *H. Middendorffiana* × *H. fulva* and described as "18 inches tall; flowers 3 inches across, 3 inner divisions orange-brown, outer divisions pointed, orange-yellow, tipped with green."

PIONEER. Described in 1899 (*Gard.* **56**: 71) as follows: "This is a seedling raised between *H. disticha* and *H. Thunbergii*, and a pretty addition to the group in question. In the form of the flower there is much to remind one of Thunberg's Daylily, and in the color there is a touch of both parents. A similar remark also applies to the foliage, that it is quite possible Pioneer will prove a somewhat interesting plant." Evidently this was one of the early hybrids between some plant of *H. fulva* and Thunberg's Daylily. Not now in the trade, at least under this name. Mr. Yeld states to the writer that he does not know the origin or the parentage of this daylily.

POLLY. Seedling from Mr. Perry. Mentioned in 1930 (*Gard. Chr.* **90**: 151) "has particularly broad and handsome foliage."

PRINCESS (plate 18). A hybrid obtained by the writer from the cross Ophir × Golden Bell. The foliage stands at a level of about 30 inches and the scapes are somewhat taller, erect, and much branched. The flowers are delicately fragrant, about five inches in spread, full with recurving segments and of a clear and uniform color slightly darker than lemon yellow. The plant is day-blooming and the period of flowering is in early July. This is the first mention of this clonal variety.

PYRRHA. In a letter to the writer in 1930, Mr. Yeld states that this daylily is small and a very pretty orange, and that he has lost record of the parentage. In 1931 (*Gard. Chr.* **89**: 425) the statement is made regarding Pyrrha that "Mr. Yeld regards it as one of the most dainty of the orange-yellow daylilies, and it is especially noteworthy for the freedom with which it produces its bloom, as many as eighteen have been counted on a single stem." The colored plate shown at this time is of the variety Sirius instead of Pyrrha as labelled.

QUEEN MARY. Mentioned in a letter from Mr. Perry in 1925. Mr. Morrison states (*Cir. 42.* 1928) that it blooms between seasons of the early and late varieties, and resembles the Meehan Daylily but has better form.

QUEEN OF MAY. This clone was received at The New York Botanical Garden from C. G. Van Tubergen in 1925. In the catalogue of V. Lemoine & Son, Nancy, France, for 1925 it was listed as a hybrid of *H. flava* × "*H. aurantiaca major.*" The foliage is evergreen, coarse, and rather robust. The scapes are coarse, erect-ascending, branched and as tall as 4 feet. The flowers are full, with a spread of over 4 inches, and their color is a uniform light cadmium or yellow-orange. The plant is in flower at The New York Botanical Garden during the first half of June, at which time it has been the tallest variety then in bloom in the collection. A note in *Horticulture* (**9**: 394), states that the flowers are fragrant and that in the District of Columbia plants of Queen of May bloom first in June and then again in autumn.

RADIANT. Seedling from Mr. Yeld. Described in 1925 (*Gard.* **89**: 421). Received Award of Merit in 1926 (*Jour. Roy. Hort. Soc.* **51**: CXIII). Half-tone illustration in *Garden Illustrated* (Aug. 11, 1929, p. 510). This plant reaches a height of 42 inches; the scapes are coarse, well branched; the flowers spread to 4–5 inches, the color is clear cadmium yellow. Blooms in July. Considered by Mr. Yeld as one of the best daylilies.

REGEL, DR. In 1904 (*Gard.* **66**: 220) this name was used in describing a "very distinct hybrid, deep orange shade, 3–4 flowers in a compact bunch and enveloped in a sheath. Flowers open quite flat in the sun." The following year this plant received an Award of Merit of the Royal Horticultural Society (*Jour Roy. Hort. Soc.* **31**: CXI) and it was stated that it possessed large flowers of a deep bronzy-yellow color. Also a note (*Gard. Chr.* **38**: 204. 1905) states that the new hybrid Dr. Regel has deep orange flowers, blooms in July and apparently has the "*H. aurantiaca major*" for a parent. After several years one finds this name listed in catalogs as the same as Middendorffiana, and also it is stated by Mr. Yeld (*Gard. Chr.* **85**: 123, 1929) that the Dr. Regel Daylily is a later flowering form of *H. Middendorffii.*

The plants which the author has received under the name Dr. Regel have definite resemblance to *H. Dumortierii.* But they are larger and more robust, with scapes more erect and about 2 feet tall; the flower is larger, somewhat darker orange in color with small faint areas of brown in the face of the petals and the foliage is strongly evergreen. The season of blooming occurs the middle part of June. I judge that this plant has *H. Dumortierii* as one parent and either *H. aurantiaca* or *H. aurantiaca* Major as the other parent. It is very distinct from plants received under the name Middendorffiana.

It seems highly probable that two rather distinct clones have been included under the name Dr. Regel: one, the hybrid that was mentioned in 1904 and 1905; the other, the clone known as Middendorffiana.

REVENGE, H. M. S. Obtained from Mr. Perry in 1931. Flower fulvous with throat and medium stripe in petals yellowish orange. Paler than Margaret Perry.

ROSE QUEEN. From Mr. Perry in 1931, who stated to the writer in 1930 that this seedling is *H. Middendorffii* crossed with some fulvous daylily, possibly Cypriana. The plant is tall with scapes to 45 inches and foliage rather erect to 35 inches. The flower is near that of the Europa Daylily in shape but is smaller and paler fulvous with throat and stripe of yellowish orange and a slight indication of an eye zone. This plant shows no trace of *H. Middendorffii* parentage.

ROYAL. Listed by Mr. Franklin B. Mead in 1925, who states in a letter to the writer that "I know practically nothing of the variety Royal except that it came direct from Japan." Mentioned by Mr. Morrison (*Cir. 42*). Plants obtained from Mr. Mead are 3 feet tall, scapes coarse, stiffly erect, flowering in July. Foliage is coarse, dark green, evergreen. Flower is 4–5 inches in spread, uniform yellow in color. Royal is similar to Luteola and also very like Shirley, but the flowers are slightly fuller.

SARACEN (THE). Obtained from Mr. Carl Purdy in 1926 who stated in a letter that it was obtained by him from C. G. Van Tubergen some ten years previous and that it closely resembles the *H. fulva* (the Europa Daylily) but is "large and strong in growth." Plants from Mr. Purdy grown by the side of the Europa Daylily from various sources show no points of difference.

SEMPERFLORENS. The author received a plant under the name Hybrida Semperflorens from C. G. Van Tubergen in 1925. The foliage is decidedly evergreen; the habit vigorous with coarse ascending scapes to a height of 40 inches. The flowers are medium large (4½ in. spread) and full, rich cadmium yellow in color. Very similar to Aureole and blooms at the same time. The Daylily Semperflorens obtained the Award of Merit of the Royal Horticultural Society in 1931.

SHEKINAH. Seedling from Mr. Perry. Noted in letter of Nov. 2, 1932 as being "3½ feet tall, broad foliage, brilliant orange scarlet, suffused orange."

SHIRLEY. Listed by the Royal Moerheim Nurseries (Dedemsvaart, Holland) and by Amos Perry as early as 1926. Origin evidently not known. Very near to Luteola. Flower slightly larger and paler. Received Award of Merit from Royal Horticultural Society in 1931. Described in 1932 (*Jour. Roy. Hort. Soc.* **57**: 108) as follows:—"Vigorous, forming dense clumps, with broad dark green arching foliage, 2 feet in height. Flower stems 3 feet tall, very branched from two-thirds of their length to the apex, 10 to 22-flowered. Flowers 5 inches diameter, flat funnel-shaped, soft pale apricot-orange, becoming darker with age, tips of petals reflexed and margins of inner petals wavy. Did not set seeds. Flowering very freely from June 12 to August 5." A different clone with the same name is also mentioned.

SIPPAN. Mentioned by Mr. Yeld in 1929 (*Gard. Chr.* **85**: 122) as from Sir Arthur Hort who in turn obtained it from H. J. Elwes, and as being "pretty but not of special distinction." Mr. Yeld states in a letter of 1930 that the plant increases very slowly.

SIR MICHAEL FOSTER. A hybrid of *H. aurantiaca* clone Major × *H. citrina;* reported by Willy Müller in 1904 (*Gard.* **66**: 121) and described by him as "Leaves evergreen, often with blue shade, elegantly recurved,at base red, grows bushy, even without flowers is a fine plant in the border. Flowers sweet-scented, clear yellow, inner petals large, undulate; outer smaller not undulate. Flower open for a day." Flowers extra large, long funnel-shaped, as much as 6 inches in spread, full with broad overlapping segments, spreading but not strongly reflexed. Strong growing, height about 4 feet. Blooms in July.

SIR WILLIAM. Seedling from Mr. Perry. Described in 1932 (*Gard. Chr.* **90**: 151) as "very showy, and of medium height with bold flowers of good form, rich orange-red, with segments conspicuously lined with yellow." In a letter Mr. Perry says "under 2 feet, rich red-terracotta, with 3 conspicuous orange lines."

SIRIUS. Mentioned in letter by Mr. Yeld in 1930 and obtained from him in 1931. Scapes come to height of 32 inches. Flowers medium full, nearly 5 inches spread; habit of flower somewhat like *H. aurantiaca;* color rich orange with tinge of fulvous. Richer in orange and less fulvous and scapes more erect than the *H. aurantiaca,* which is evidently one of the parents. Awarded A. M. from Royal Horticultural Society in 1931. A flower of Sirius was illustrated in the *Gardeners' Chronicle* (**89**: 425. 1931) under the name Pyrrha.

SOUDAN (plate 22). A sister seedling to Vesta and Wau-Bun. First described and illustrated in halftone in 1932 (*Jour. N. Y. Bot. Garden* **33**: 104–105). The Soudan Daylily somewhat resembles the old popular Lemon Daylily (*Hemerocallis flava*), but it blooms in New York in July after the former is entirely through flowering. In comparison with the Lemon Daylily the plant is somewhat larger, the scapes are taller, and the flowers have broader petals making a fuller flower; but in general color and size, the flowers are nearly the same. Hence those who are fond of the Lemon Daylily will find the Soudan Daylily of interest and value in continuing this class of plant and flower into the midsummer season. The foliage of the Soudan Daylily is medium coarse, medium dark green, and ascending to a general level of about two feet. The scapes about three feet tall, branching, nearly erect, and holding the flowers well above the leaves. The flowers are clear empire-yellow in color and gold-glistening; the petals have somewhat wavy margins, and they are wide and overlapping, making an unusually full flower with a spread of about four and a half inches. The plant is day-blooming, very floriferous, and summer-flowering.

SOVEREIGN. This clone is almost a duplicate of the Gold Dust Daylily in habit of growth and season of bloom, but the flowers are paler with more yellow and less orange in the coloring. Mr. Yeld states in 1906 (*Third Int. Conf. Genetics*, p. 415) that

Plate 22. *Above,* Soudan Daylily. *Below,* Winsome Daylily

Plate 23. Flower of Taruga Daylily

Plate 24. Flower of Theron Daylily

this variety was then in the trade. Received Award of Merit of Royal Horticultural Society in 1931.

SPRENGERI. Listed by Fairmont Iris Gardens in 1932.

STAHL, PROFESSOR. See under Gold Ball.

STOKER, MARY. Seedling from Mr. Perry. Described in 1932 (*Gard. Chr.* **90**: 151) as "bold handsome flowers of reddish-orange, lined with sulphur yellow and with an orange base."

SUNKIST. Noted by Mrs. Nesmith in 1932 (*Hort.* **9**: 292) as "deep soft rose, 3½ feet Aug. 1–25, large flower." Described in 1932 (*Gard. Chr.* **90**: 151) as having "flowers of perfect form with broad overlapping petals, the inner petals soft rosy-bronze, and the outer sepals yellow, faintly flushed with rose, and with an orange base." Listed in autumn catalog, 1932 by Mr. Perry as "This pretty form is about 2 feet high bearing a profusion of medium-sized well-formed flowers, petals broad and enveloping, a pretty shade of bronzy-rose, inner petals yellow, faintly flushed rose; very free."

SUNNY WEST. Noted by Mrs. Nesmith in 1932 (*Hort.* **9**: 292) as "lovely yellow, 2½ feet, August 1–15, August 1–25, large flower." Produced by Mr. H. P. Sass who states in a letter that it is a seedling of *H. citrina* crossed with *H. aurantiaca* clone Major.

SUNSET. Seedling of Amos Perry. Described in 1932 (*Gard. Chr.* **90**: 151) as "a glowing shade of crimson-copper, the inner segments conspicuously lined, a distinct and unique variety."

TANGERINE (see plate 17). In 1906 (*Rep. Third Conf. Genetics*, p. 415) Mr. Yeld states that record of the parentage of Tangerine was lost. The writer obtained plants of Tangerine from Mr. Perry in 1926. The plant is close to *H. Middendorffii* in general habit, but is seldom more than 20 inches tall in ordinary garden soil. The scapes are ascending in all directions from the crown, with the flowers only slightly above the tips of the leaves. The flowers are slightly fuller and darker orange than the

H. Middendorffii and the buds are tinged with red. In the spreading scapes, red flower buds, and plump rounded capsules, Tangerine shows characters of *H. Dumortierii.* It is very similar to the hybrids which the author has raised from *H. Dumortierii* × *H. Middendorffii.* An excellent variety; semi-dwarf; early-flowering; rich orange. Received Award of Merit of Royal Horticultural Society in 1931.

TAPLOW ORANGE. Described in 1932 (*Jour. Roy. Hort. Soc.* **57**: 109) as "Vigorous; forming close tufts of medium green foliage, which droops towards the tips, 2 feet tall. Flower stems 3½ feet tall, closely and sparsely branched near the summit; erect; 6- to 8-flowered. Flowers 4 inches diameter, almost cup-shaped, not opening widely in dull weather, bright orange-apricot. Seeds of medium size, sparingly produced in short oval capsules. Flowering from June 17 to July 13."

TAPLOW YELLOW. Observed at Wisley in 1930; from Barr and Sons. Described in 1932 (*Jour. Roy. Hort. Soc.* **57**: 108) as "very similar to Semperflorens in habit; the foliage is much paler and the flowers flatter, smaller, and less freely borne. Flowering from June 22 to July 16."

TARUGA (plate 23). First described and flower illustrated in 1933 (*Hort.* **11**: 27). The plant has erect well-branched scapes about three feet tall. The flower is widely spreading to a width of about six inches. The petals are long, somewhat narrow, and noticeably twisted and folded. The color is a clear lemon-yellow with a very faint and hardly noticeable tinge of fulvous in the midzone. Compared with Wau-Bun, which is its seed parent, the flowers are less full, the color is more nearly yellow, the period of flowering is later (July), and the plant is somewhat taller. Selected by Mrs. Barnabas Bryan Jr., in 1931 as an outstanding plant among numerous fine seedlings with large flowers developed at The New York Botanical Garden.

THERON (plate 24). The outstanding feature of the Theron Daylily is the dark red coloring of its flowers. The throat of the flower is pale yellowish orange with shades of green at the extreme base, but outside of the throat the color is dark red of a shade that approaches mahogany red. When the flowers first open and on days of reduced sunlight the color approaches black or purplish black. The flowers are of good size, fairly full, spreading, and day-blooming. The seedling is now two years old and probably not developed to its full stature, but thus far the height of the scapes has been about 30 inches. The foliage is ample and ascending-spreading. The scapes are erect, branched above, and they hold the flowers well above the leaves. The period of flowering is July. Selected and named by Mrs. Theron G. Strong, a member of the Advisory Council of The New York Botanical Garden.

The above is a part of the first description of this daylily published in 1934 (*Gard. Chr.* **95**: 43. figure 18) together with an illustration of the flower.

URMIENSIS. Observed in Mr. Yeld's garden in 1930. Small plant; flower small, clear yellow-orange, with brown back. This plant was given to Mr. Yeld by Sir Arthur Hort. Mentioned by Mr. Yeld in *Gard. Chr.* **85**: 122. 1929.

VESTA. A sister seedling of Wau-Bun and Soudan. First described with photographs of the plant and of the flowers in *House and Garden* in 1929 (**55**: 126); also described with the same illustrations in *Jour. New York Botanical Garden* in 1931 (**32**: 30). The plant has a compact habit of growth with scapes about 30 inches tall. The flowers (see plate 31) have a spread of about 4½ inches, the petals and sepals are broad and overlapping and their color is deep orange with a slight trace of fulvous in the midzone. Vesta blooms in late June and early July.

VISCOUNTESS BYNG. Seedling from Mr. Perry. Described in 1931 (*Gard. Chr.* **90**: 151) as "flowers of medium size and perfect form, with full overlapping petals, pale citron yellow, flushed and lined with apricot and yellow at the base; the height being 2½ feet." In the catalog of Amos Perry for autumn 1932 it is stated that the foliage is thin and grass-like and the scapes are slender. Mrs. Thomas Nesmith states (*Hort.* **10**: 291. 1932) that the flower is pale coppery rose, open, and of good size.

VOMERENSE. Hybrid from Charles Sprenger and Willy Müller, said to be *H. Thunbergii* × "*H. minor crocea.*" Described in 1903 by Sprenger (*Gard. Chr.* **34**: 122). Slender grass-like foliage; flower segments narrow, color yellowish-orange.

VULCAN (plate 25). Selected by the author as an outstanding seedling with rich and sprightly shades of dark red coloring in the flowers. The throat of the flower has a greenish tinge over cadmium yellow; outside of the throat the face of the petals is maroon with a slightly darker midzone, and the back of the petals is also strongly colored: the sepals are uniformly maroon on the inner face but red only along the margins on the reverse. The petals are somewhat twisting and the sepals are stiffly recurving. The flower has a spread of over five inches. The season for flowering is in early July. On account of repeated division for propagation well-established plants of Vulcan have not been had but the stature of such plants will probably be robust. In the selective breeding that gave Vulcan a seedling of Luteola × *H. aurantiaca* was crossed with a richly colored fulvous daylily obtained by crossing *H. fulva* var. *rosea* with a wild plant of *H. fulva* from China.

WAU–BUN (plate 32). First described and illustrated in 1929 (*House and Garden* **55**: 126). A colored plate and rather complete description appeared in 1930 (*Addisonia* **15**: plate 488). When well developed the plant is of semi-robust stature; the foliage is evergreen and reaches a level of about 30 inches, and the scapes are ascending rather than erect and are several inches above the foliage. The flower is of large size for daylilies; the sepals are broad and stiffly recurving; the petals are broad, spreading rather than recurving, and in the outer half they are folded backward along the midrib and also somewhat twisted near the tip. The color of both sepals and petals is a shade of yellow classed as light cadmium over which there is a delicate sprinkling of very faint fulvous. The period of blooming is late June into

July. An unusual form of flower owing to the folded and twisted character of the petals, large size of flower, rich yellow coloring, and a good habit of growth give this clone much individual charm as a plant for the flower garden. The Winnebago Indian name Wau-Bun, which signifies the early morn with its rising sun, has been chosen as a suitable horticultural name for this hybrid daylily.

WINSOME (plate 22). Seedling from George Yeld mentioned in 1925 (*Gard.* **89**: 379). Obtained Award of Merit in 1930 from Royal Horticultural Society by unanimous vote (*Jour. Roy. Hort. Soc.* **51**: XIX). In 1930 Mr. Yeld told the writer that he considered this the best of all his hybrids. The plant is semi-robust; scapes to 30 inches, rather stiffly erect and branched. Flowers full, wide-spreading, 3½ inches diameter, color between empire yellow and cadmium yellow, reverse tinged with brownish red. Blooms early, beginning about May 25, overlapping the flowering of such varieties as of Apricot, Gold Dust, and Sovereign. Flower paler than Apricot and somewhat larger.

WYMAN, DONALD (or D. D. WYMAN). Listed by Carl Betscher and by Bay State Nurseries in 1929. Scapes to 34 inches, with flowers only slightly above leaves. Flower large with spread of about 6 inches and pale fulvous; widely spreading but lacks fullness.

WYMAN, MRS. W. H. For a time called Latest. Seedling from Mr. Betscher. Listed in 1929. Plants robust; scapes coarse branching to 40 inches. Flowers medium large (about 5 inches), spreading recurving, medium full; color near light cadmium, almost same as Luteola, but flower larger and plant taller. Said to be "extremely late flowering" but at the New York Botanical Garden, thus far, the period of flowering has been confined to July.

YELD, GEORGE. A seedling reared by Mr. Amos Perry and said to be a hybrid of *H. Thunbergii* × *H. fulva* clone Cypriana. Offered to the trade in 1926. This daylily has large open flowers fully six inches across, with pale fulvous coloring.

YELLOW HAMMER. Listed by Mr. Perry in the autumn of 1925 as a new seedling. Plants obtained from him in 1926 are 3 feet tall with foliage vigorous and erect-ascending. Flowers large, tubular, medium full, light cadmium (orange-yellow). Blooms in July; night-flowering, on hot days the flowers are almost closed at 10:00 A.M.

Plate 25. Flower of Vulcan Daylily

Plate 26. Daylilies of different stature, all in same scale. *H. Dumortierii*, semi-dwarf; Lemon Daylily, semi-robust; Maculata Daylily and wild plant of *H. fulva*, robust; wild plant of unnamed type, giant; inset, *H. nana*, dwarf.

CHAPTER VII

AN EVALUATION OF THE DAYLILIES

In the preceding chapter the clonal varieties of daylilies are arranged alphabetically and the data regarding the individual characters and the origin are presented with, in many cases, some remarks regarding their merits. It was the aim to list all clonal varieties that have been named. Some of these clones are no longer in culture or even in existence. Others are of no special merit; evidently some of these were named when few daylilies were known or when there were few seedlings from which to make selections. Certain varieties are very similar to each other and differ in only minor characters, and the choice between them calls for close comparison.

Rating. Thus far no official rating has been applied to the various clones of daylilies except that the Royal Horticultural Society has, for about 40 years, judged various daylilies submitted for consideration and for test in the trial grounds of the Society and has granted a "First Class Certificate," an "Award of Garden Merit," or the rating "Highly Commended" to various of them.

During the years 1929–1931 the Royal Horticultural Society obtained 117 stocks of *Hemerocallis* for culture in the gardens of the Society at Wisley. Of these, the "Award of Merit" was bestowed on *H. flava, H. Dumortierii, H. Middendorffii, H. aurantiaca* clone Major, *H. fulva* clone Flore Pleno, "*H. disticha flore pleno,*" and the clones Apricot, Aureole, J. S. Gayner, Lady Fermoy Hesketh, Hyperion, Marigold, Margaret Perry, Ophir, Radiant, Semperflorens, Shirley, Sovereign, and Sirius. The rating "Highly Commended" was given to Ajax, Gold Standard, Golden Bell, Ochroleuca, Queen of May, and *H. Thunbergii.*

But there are, in addition to these, many excellent daylilies both among the older varieties and among the clones of recent origin, many of which have not been grown at Wisley. Also several of those mentioned above are without doubt surpassed by some of the newer varieties and some of the more recent clonal varieties are distinctly new in respect to certain characters.

Selection according to class. In selecting the best types of daylilies for culture one will recognize that the horticultural clones have now become so numerous and so diversified that consideration in respect to their most important garden qualities is desirable and useful in making comparisons and selections. Attention may first be directed to such important features as (1) the habits of flowering, (2) the color of flowers, and (3) the stature and habits of growth. Odor of flowers is a quality of interest to many. On the basis of any one of these outstanding qualities, daylilies fall into somewhat well-defined classes or groups. Within each group further evaluation and selection may be made according to diversity, to points of individual and special merit, and to personal preferences.

Stature of Daylilies

The stature of daylilies is determined chiefly by the height which the flower branches reach. But there is also the height and form of the mound of foliage for this determines the stature before and after the flowering period. Also in the types with drooping scapes and in clones in which the scapes are only slightly above the leaves (see plates 9, 10, 12, and 13) the foliage dominates in the stature even when the plants are in flower. Stature is a feature of importance for it largely determines where a variety is to be placed, especially in a mixed perennial border. In general the stature of the various daylilies may be considered as falling into the five somewhat arbitrary classes considered in the following paragraphs.

In plate 26 several daylilies representing these classes in stature are shown side by side in the *same* scale. Also the plates 2, 3, 5 and 10 are all reproduced on a scale of one inch to a foot

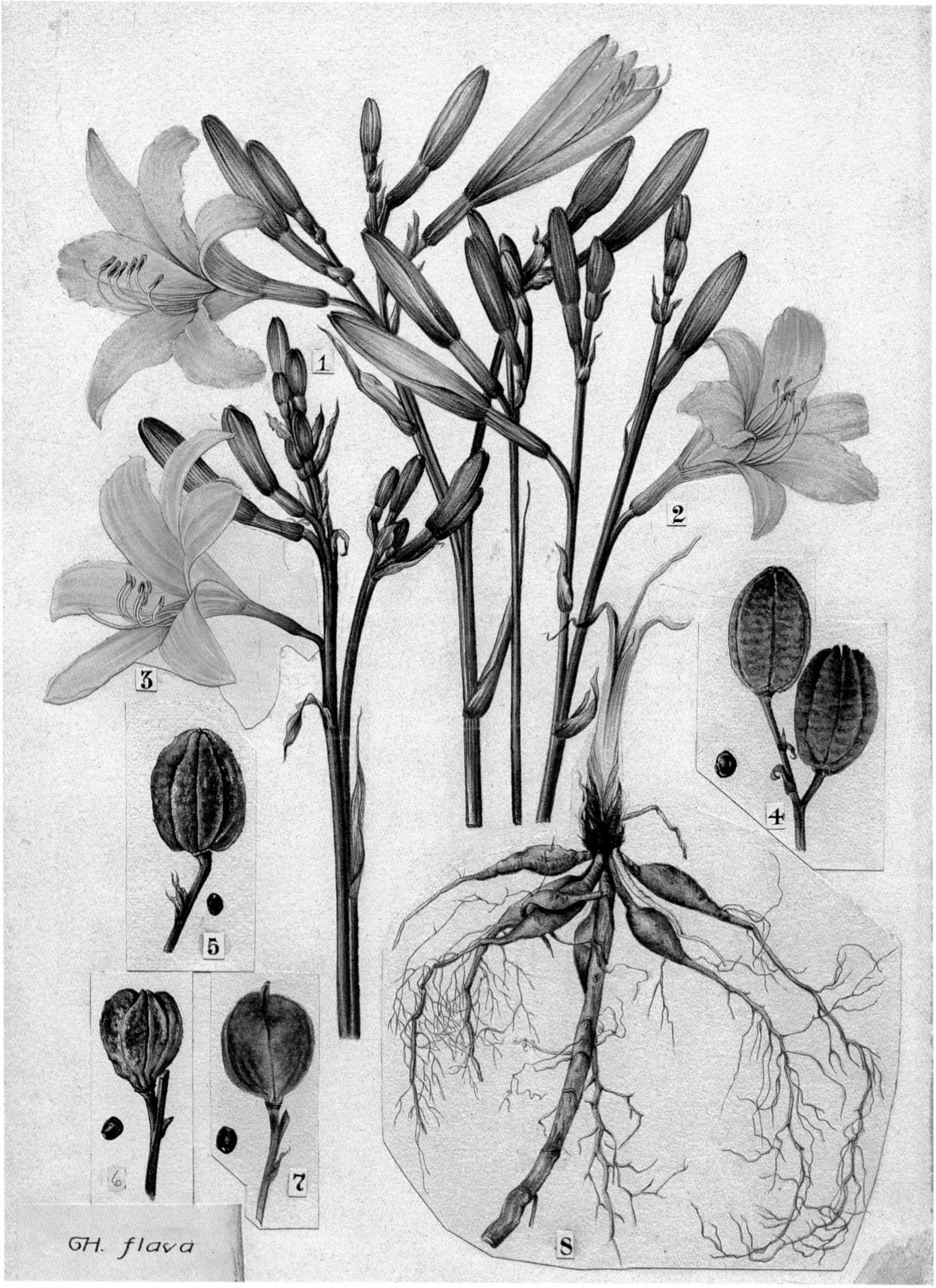

V. The Lemon Daylily is the most popular early, yellow-flowered species in landscapes today. Its blooms are borne on thirty-six inch scapes, are pleasantly fragrant, and stay open into the second day. Plants form thick clumps and spread by rhizomes. *Courtesy of The New York Botanical Garden Library.*

VI. The Many-flowered Daylily was described and illustrated by A. B. Stout in *Addisonia* (14: plate 464) in 1929. Scapes reach forty inches in height and bend from the weight of as many as one hundred flowers. The blooms continue over a long period, with some forms starting in late July, others in August and September. *Courtesy of The New York Botanical Garden Library.*

VII. *Hemerocallis fulva* exhibits many different flower forms and colors. The first form of this species to come to America was *H. fulva* 'Europa'; it was a nonbreeding, sterile triploid. A. B. Stout collected many other representatives of the genus for his breeding program. He found that the brownish yellow color of the species varied and included pink (*H. fulva* var. *rosea*) and brownish red (*H. fulva* var. *longituba*). *Courtesy of The New York Botanical Garden Library.*

VIII. Thunberg's Daylily blooms shortly after the Tawny Daylily. Flower scapes are forty-five inches tall and well branched. Flowers tend to fade and wilt during hot afternoons. The below-ground portions of leaf bases are either white or pink. *Courtesy of The New York Botanical Garden Library.*

IX. Most pink daylilies are descendants of the true botanical variety *Hemerocallis fulva* var. *rosea*. Rosalind (right, second from top), a seedling of two *H. fulva rosea* parents, was widely distributed. Rosalind was the parent of over one hundred different progenies like those shown. Charmaine (upper left corner) was one of the early pink selections and was also used extensively in hybridizing for pink. *Courtesy of The New York Botanical Garden Library.*

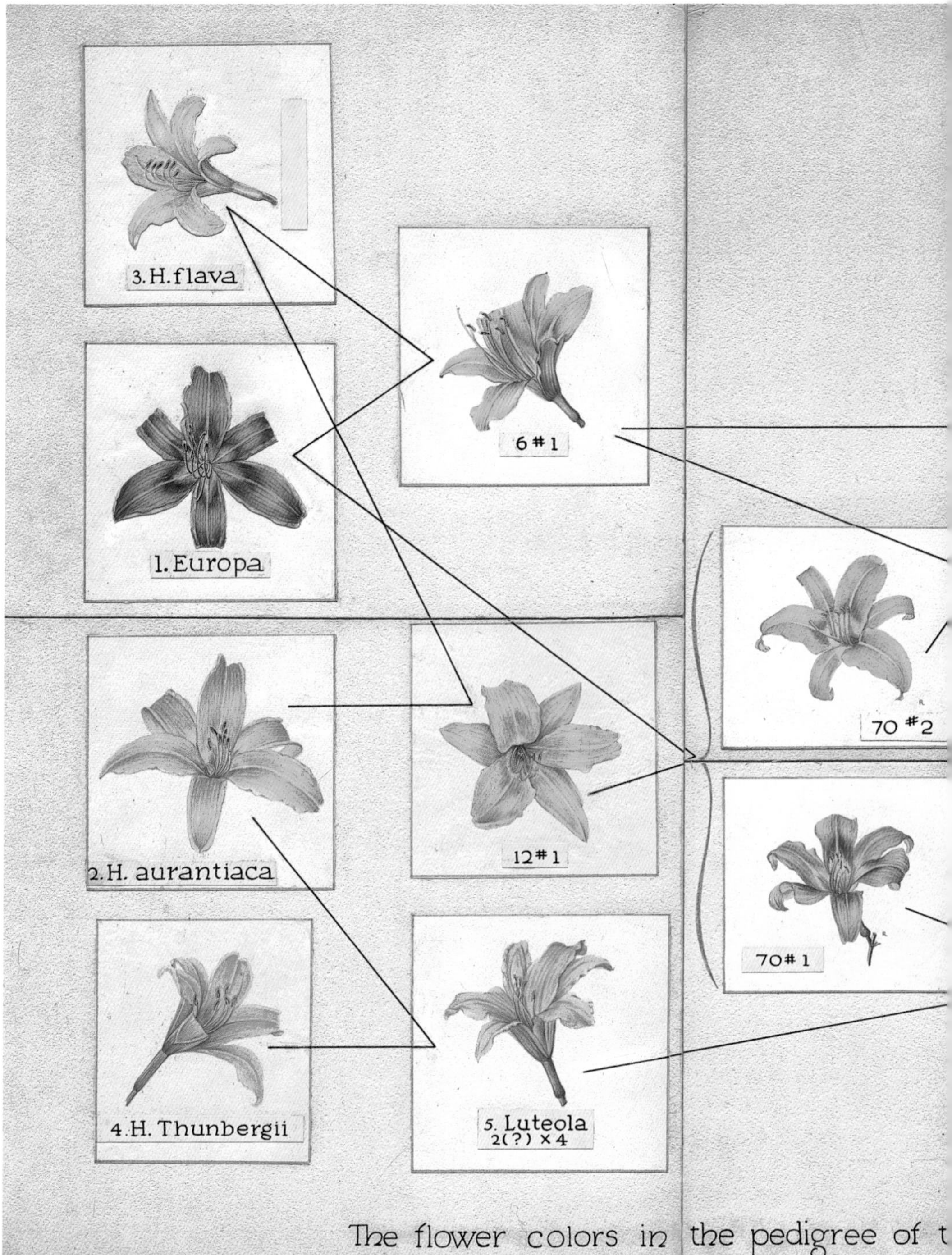

The flower colors in the pedigree of t

A climax in selective breeding for dark red color, 'Theron', the first truly red daylily, was produced by Dr. Stout and described in 1934. Four different species and eight selection seedlings were involved in the ancestry. It took twenty-five years of painstaking work.
eron type of Daylily

X. The Theron Daylily represented a new combination of genetic factors with intensified pigmentation in both the mid- and distal portions of the flower. The red pigmentation is from *Hemerocallis aurantiaca* and *H. fulva* 'Europa'. Quite possibly, the genes for color intensification are from *H. flava* and/or *H. thunbergii*. A description and drawing of the cultivar was first published in the January 1934 *Gardeners' Chronical*. Its outstanding feature was the dark mahogany red coloring of its flowers, which on dark cloudy days appear black or purplish black. This color is not approached in any of the known species of *Hemerocallis*. *Courtesy of The New York Botanical Garden Library.*

XI. The blooms of Dumortier's Daylily are displayed at ascending angles and open with *Hemerocallis flava* and *H. minor*. The outside of the flowers is strongly tinged with brown. Plants are usually less than two feet tall with unbranched scapes. *Courtesy of The New York Botanical Garden Library.*

of the plant. A comparison of these plates will give the reader an idea of the relative sizes of the plants which are to be had in daylilies.

The dwarf class—including, let us consider, those daylilies that are not more than one foot tall—has special promise of charm and value in rock gardens and in the foreground of the mixed border of perennials.

Of the older horticultural clones the writer has seen only one which has this dwarf stature (see plate 27) and this closely resembles *H. Dumortierii.* There are also the species *H. Forrestii, H. nana* (plates 4 and 26), and *H. plicata,* of which, according to herbarium specimens of wild plants, some are often less than a foot tall. But in cultivation, plants of *H. nana* may be as many as sixteen inches tall. Mr. Yeld has reported two seedlings, named Moidore and Miniken, that have *H. nana* as one parent, and Miniken is described as "dwarf." The writer now has numerous first generation hybrids of *H. flava* × *H. nana,* but these are not dwarf. A seedling that seems to be dwarf has been named Nada (see plate 27). Several seedlings of dwarf stature obtained from other parentage are being propagated and good varieties in the dwarf class are certain to appear in the future.

The semi-dwarf class, with flower stalks standing from one to two feet tall, includes a number of types that are early-flowering and which have either yellow- or orange-colored flowers. This list includes the species *H. Dumortierii* (plates 10 and 11), or at least the more robust type of this species, *H. minor* (plate 2), the clones called *H. gracilis, H. Middendorffii* (plate 10), and such excellent clonal varieties as Tangerine, Estmere, Orangeman, Gold Dust, Sovereign, and Apricot (see plates 12, 13 and 17). But in rich soil, well-established plants of several of these reach the height of 30 inches. For these there are noteworthy differences in the habits of growth. In Estmere the foliage is recurving and the scapes spreading-ascending. In Tangerine the foliage is more erect and the scapes spreading. In Gold Dust and Sovereign the foliage is rather erect and the scapes are erect and taller than the leaves. In Apricot the tips of the nearly erect leaves may extend slightly above the flowers. All of these bloom early. There are very few clones of semi-dwarf stature now in the trade that bloom in midsummer. The late or autumn flowering species *H. multiflora* has plants about two feet tall. Of the newer varieties, Perry's Pigmy is described as only 18 inches tall and Sir William and Sunkist as not over two feet tall.

Of *the semi-robust class,* standing between two and three feet tall, there are many daylilies that are good or excellent. For early flowering there is the Lemon Daylily (plates 2 and 26) which stands at a height of 3 feet. For June there are Ajax, Dr. Regel, Aureole, Winsome, and Modesty. For late June into July there is Wau-Bun, and slightly later there are Vesta, Luteola, Majestic, Shirley, Royal, Cinnabar, Bijou, Taruga, Anna Betscher, Sirius, and the species *H. aurantiaca.* In these the scapes are erect or nearly so and the flowers stand above the foliage, but there are some noticeable differences in the relative height of the foliage and the scapes, and also in the character of the foliage.

In *the robust class,* standing let us say from over three feet to about five feet tall, there are many sorts which present a wide variety of flower colors. The scapes are erect and usually well above the foliage which in most cases is robust. In this class is Queen of May which flowers in New York in early June and also Parthenope which flowers somewhat later. Nearly all of the most robust daylilies now in the trade bloom in midsummer and include *H. Thunbergii,* H. citrina, various clones of *H. fulva,* and numerous named clonal varieties as Ophir, Sir Michael Foster, Mikado, Jubilee, Princess, Hyperion, Lady Fermoy Hesketh, Radiant, Soudan, Lemona, and Margaret Perry.

A giant class, composed of types with scapes more than five feet tall, may be expected in the future. The writer has daylilies (see plate 26) over seven feet tall in wild plants of a pale yellow night-flowering type that are of no merit as garden plants but which are being used in breeding in the effort to develop giant types of merit.

Plate 27. *Above,* dwarf plant resembling *H. Dumortierii* with 6-inch rule. *Below,* Nada Daylily, with a foot rule

Plate 28. Ophir Daylily. Upper parts of plant and yard stick shown

The Colors of Flowers

The species of daylilies fall into three main classes in respect to flower colors; yellow, orange, and fulvous-colored. But in the numerous hybrid clones the colors have been diversified and extended into almost every possible shade of yellow and orange both in clear colors and in combination with shades of fulvous and red. Hence a grouping under the three classes mentioned above is not fully satisfactory or adequate for the horticultural clones. Yet these main classes in respect to color may be retained as somewhat useful in descriptions and comparisons.

Yellow and orange-colored daylilies. The hybrids of the yellow and the orange-colored early-blooming species, *H. flava, M. minor, H. Dumortierii* and *H. Middendorffii,* are yellow or orange, and of these Tangerine, Apricot, Estmere, Gold Dust, and Orangeman are of special merit. Several of these have a brownish red coloring on the flower buds which continues as a rather conspicuous feature on the reverse of the sepals after the flowers open. Modesty is pale yellow, Winsome slightly darker yellow, and Queen of May light orange, all flowering in June. Of the clones which have clear yellow or orange shades of color and which bloom in midsummer, mention may be made of Luteola, Shirley, Parthenope, Amber, Marigold, Sir Michael Foster, Ophir, Soudan, Taruga, Hyperion, Lemona, Anna Betscher, Radiant, Royal, Majestic, and Princess. The last nine named are of recent origin.

Fulvous daylilies. Many of the hybrids between fulvous daylilies (especially of the *H. aurantiaca*) and clear yellow and orange-colored types have only a faint or sparse development of fulvous colors in the face of the open flower that is often scarcely noticeable. Of the older varieties Ajax and Aureole are of this class. Wau-Bun and Vesta have, also, only traces of fulvous coloring. Sirius is rich orange in ground color with a faint tinge of fulvous similar to, but less fulvous than, *H. aurantiaca.*

Fulvous daylilies of species or older horticultural origin include the *H. aurantiaca, H. fulva* clon Europa, *H. fulva* clon Maculata and a new type with rosy-pink coloring called *H. fulva* var. *rosea.* Good strongly colored fulvous daylilies of hybrid origin have only appeared recently and the best of these are of special interest to gardeners. There is George Yeld with large flowers rather yellowish orange with a moderate flush of fulvous overcast. The flowers of Margaret Perry have a throat of yellowish orange which extends out through the fulvous colored petals and sepals making a charming pattern. Mr. Amos Perry has recently named and briefly described several new seedlings that have fulvous colors including Dawn, Shekinah, Sunkist, Gladys Perry, Imperator, and Byng of Vimy. Cinnabar has a much richer fulvous coloring than the *H. aurantiaca.* Bijou has rather small flowers of a rich and sprightly fulvous coloring. Charmaine has flowers of a clear rosy-pink; the first of this type named by the author. The Mikado has flowers with a large blotch of dark mahogany red in each petal which forms a pattern of bold contrasts somewhat new and outstanding. Jubilee has a conspicuous eye zone in a flower rather yellow. Another hybrid, Theron, has a throat of pale yellow-orange outside of which the color is a dark red of a shade that approaches mahogany red. This is a distinctly new coloring for a daylily. Vulcan has dark rich maroon colors. Nada is a dwarf plant with flowers morocco red in color.

In addition to the new clones already mentioned, the writer has at the present time at least 100 seedlings in a wide range of fulvous, rosy pink, red, and mahogany-red colorings in solid colors and in eyed patterns that are plants of special merit. Certain of these have been selected for propagation and possibly for future introduction.

The Flowering Habits of Daylilies

The flowering habits of a daylily have an important bearing on its value as a garden plant. *First,* there is the behavior of the individual flowers as to the period of day or night when they are open and most attractive. Some varieties are so decidedly night-blooming that they are of little use in the garden. *Second,* there is the matter of the season when a variety flowers. This is to be considered in selecting varieties that will provide a succession of flowers throughout the long season when it is possible to have daylilies in flower. *Third*, there is the question of the amount of bloom. A few varieties are shy in the production of flowers while others are especially prolific. Due consideration is to be given to such points as these in judging the merits of the different daylilies.

Habits of opening. Among daylilies there are three main types of behavior in respect to the time of the day when flowers first spread their petals and to the length of the period during which they remain open and fresh. For one group of daylilies the flowers are, in normal behavior, strictly *daylight-blooming* or *diurnal*. Another group is chiefly *night-blooming* or *nocturnal* and have open flowers during daylight only when there is cool or cloudy weather. There is also the *extended-blooming*, in which flowers may be open for a period of more than twenty-four hours.

The day-blooming class. Of the older types in cultivation the Europa Daylily is strictly day-blooming. Usually at the hour of daybreak none of its flowers are open and, as a rule, not until an hour or so later do flowers start their anthesis. Nearly always the flowers close before sundown. The name "*Hemerocallis*," bestowed in 1753 by the botanist Linneaus as the generic name for the natural group of daylilies and still so used, means in the Greek derivation "beautiful for a day." But before that date, writers recorded that the daylilies then known were commonly called "Ephemeron" and "Hemerocallis" which, we may note, are quite the same in meaning as the modern appellation "daylily." *H. aurantiaca*, *H. Dumortierii* and *H. Middendorffii* are day-blooming.

Night-blooming daylilies. The habit of blooming only during the hours of darkness is strongly developed in *H. citrina*. At The New York Botanical Garden, plants of this daylily are in flower during July and August, and on most days the flowers are either entirely closed or are only partly open during the hours of strongest daylight. Varieties, such as Calypso, Baroni, Ochroleuca, Citronella, Gold Standard, and Gold Imperial, that are evidently derived from breeding with *H. citrina*, are also most frequently night-blooming or the flowers tend to open most widely during the hours of darkness. During a series of hot days, these varieties often have their flowers entirely closed at the hour of 10:00 A.M., and the plants stand in this condition at least until late afternoon when a new set of flowers may start to open.

Extended blooming. The flowers of the Lemon Daylily (*H. flava*) are more lasting than those of most other daylilies and they are also somewhat more variable in respect to the hours of opening. But this may be owing in part to the fact that *H. flava* begins to bloom almost a month earlier than *H. fulva.* During cool weather, flowers of *H. flava* often open during the hours of late afternoon and remain open and in good condition throughout the next day and the night following. But the most usual behavior for this daylily is for flowers to open before daylight and to continue fresh until some time during the following night, in which case the period of the anthesis is almost a combination of the nocturnal and the diurnal periods and hence it may be termed "extended blooming." The overlap of different sets of flowers is such that during most of its season of flowering a plant of *H. flava* will have some flowers open at any time of the day or the night.

For Thunberg's Daylily the flowers normally open in the evening but they usually last throughout the next day. When there are periods of hot weather the flowers often fade and wilt or even close during the afternoon.

In respect to flowering habits the best sorts of daylilies are those that are very consistently daylight-blooming in every sort of weather, with flowers that hold form, color, and freshness throughout the hours of daylight even during days of high temperatures. Then the succession of different sets of flowers provide flowers day after day over the entire period of blooming. The long list of the varieties with this flowering habit include Orangeman, Estmere, Tangerine, Apricot, Gold Dust, Sovereign, Aureole, Winsome, Sirius, Wau-Bun, Parthenope, Sir Michael Foster, Luteola, Shirley, Soudan, Radiant, Royal, Ophir, Mikado, and Vesta.

Plate 29. *Above*, flowers of *H. citrina* which are nocturnal. *Below*, *H. flava* which has extended blooming: (1) old flowers and (2) new flowers open at the same time

Plate 30. Flowers of the Gold Dust Daylily. *A*, at 10 A.M.; *B*, at 2 P.M. A set of older flowers (at 1) and a set of newer flowers (at 2) are open together during the afternoon

Occasionally on certain varieties and during cool weather a set of flowers will last for two days and on the second day a new set of flowers may open. This condition is shown in plate 29 for the Lemon Daylily and in plate 30 for the Gold Dust Daylily. In such cases the older flowers are usually darker in color. It will add to the total display of color which daylilies make in the garden, and to the value of daylilies as cut flowers, if types can be developed whose flowers habitually remain open and attractive for a period of several days.

Season of Flowering

Records of the periods of flowering for daylilies growing at The New York Botanical Garden have been kept for several years. There is considerable variation from year to year, even for a single plant of a species or a variety, in respect to the calendar dates of the first and the last flowers, the extent of the period of bloom, and the climax of flowering.

For example, the same plant of *H. flava* (Lemon Daylily) began flowering in 1928 on May 22, in 1929 on May 8, and in 1930 on May 17. The clone Orangeman began bloom in 1928 on May 25, in 1929 on May 1, and in 1930 on May 31. Thus the dates of first bloom, last bloom, and climax of flowering frequently vary for the same plant from year to year by as many as 10 to 15 days.

Also the dates of relative blooming of various species and varieties are not the same from year to year even for the same well-established plants grown side by side. In 1928 the *H. flava* was the first daylily to open a flower in the experimental plots; in 1929 Orangeman and Gold Dust were first; in 1930 and 1933 *H. Middendorffii* and *H. minor* were first. Such variations are also seen for daylilies which flower later in the season and they probably arise from differences in weather and in the relative development of the plants. Small divisions have few flowers and a short period of bloom but as the plants become established and increase in spread the number of flowers increases and the period of bloom is more extended.

The calendar dates of bloom will of course vary in different countries according to climate and also in the different latitudes of a single country like the United States. In Cuba the Europa Daylily thrives and is in bloom from April into June while about New York City plants of this same clone are not usually in flower until about July 1st.

But the different species and the clonal varieties have rather definite seasons for flowering that are to be considered in selecting varieties. The following chart indicates what the periods of bloom have been during two or more years at The New York Botanical Garden for well-established plants of most of the species and for some of the best varieties. In this chart the lines indicate the periods of flowering for various single clones and the dots indicate the period of flowering of several seedlings or clones belonging in a single species.

Four species and the hybrids between them are *early-flowering* and these are usually through bloom by the middle of June. Then there is an interval of about ten days before the summer-blooming species *H. aurantiaca* and *H. Thunbergii* show flowers. During this interim, however, several good varieties are in flower which, it appears, are hybrids having both early-flowering and summer-flowering types in their ancestry. Of these Ajax, Winsome, Modesty, Aureole, Queen of May, and Wau-Bun may be noted.

The various cultivated clones and wild plants at present grouped under the name *H. fulva* differ somewhat in periods of blooming. The clone Europa starts flowering about July 1 and is through before August 1st. The double-flowered types and the clone Maculata come into flower later. Some sixty wild plants of *H. fulva* obtained from Japan and China bloom chiefly between July 10 to September 1st, with differences as to exact dates. One fulvous daylily closely resembling the Europa in appearance has flowered heavily during August and then continued to yield some flowers until the time of freezing temperatures in November.

The cultivated clone of *H. citrina* blooms from the latter part of July throughout most of August.

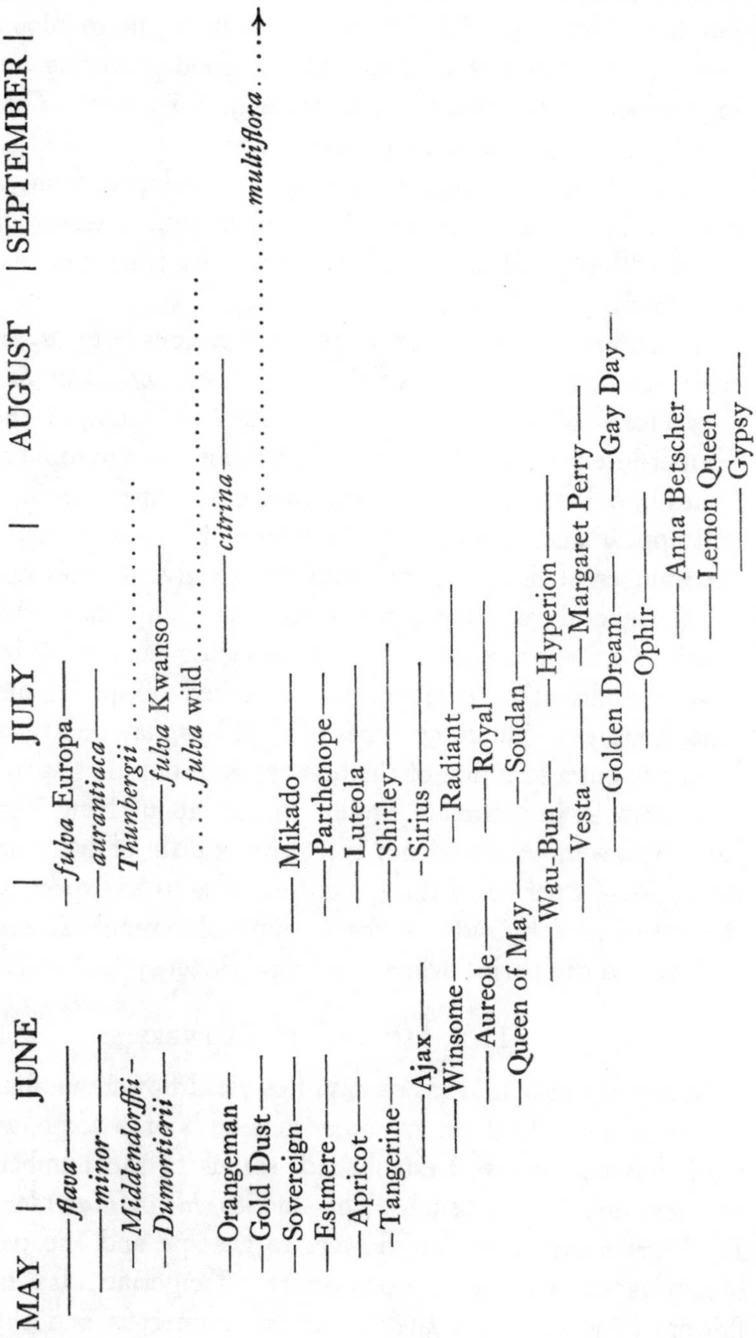
MAY
JUNE
JULY
AUGUST
SEPTEMBER
flava
minor
Middendorffi
Dumortierii
fulva Europa
aurantiaca
Thunbergii
fulva Kwanso
fulva wild
citrina
multiflora
Orangeman
Gold Dust
Sovereign
Estmere
Apricot
Tangerine
Mikado
Parthenope
Luteola
Shirley
Sirius
Ajax
Winsome
Radiant
Aureole
Royal
Queen of May
Soudan
Wau-Bun
Hyperion
Vesta
Margaret Perry
Golden Dream
Gay Day
Ophir
Anna Betscher
Lemon Queen
Gypsy

Two plants of *H. multiflora* regularly bloom during August, but the others thus far obtained usually begin to bloom about September 1st and several continue in good flowering until killing temperatures occur, often as late as in November. This species is to be classed as *autumn-flowering*.

Each of the horticultural clones is developed from a single plant and hence any one clone has a more limited season of bloom than a collection of different individuals of a species or of a group of hybrids.

A habit of *second-flowering* is seen in various hybrids, and especially for certain hybrids which have *H. aurantiaca* or *H. aurantiaca* clone Major in their ancestry. For example the clone Semperflorens begins flowering about the middle of June and continues into July, then in late summer new scapes bearing flowers will appear and continue the flowering throughout autumn, but the number of flowers is not sufficient to give a good display of color. Several varieties and numerous seedlings have this habit, which is an approach to an ever-flowering condition, but none have it sufficiently developed to be ranked of special merit. In time, good ever-blooming types of daylilies may be available.

At present a selection of the best types of daylilies available for gardens will, in a climate similar to that about New York City, furnish flowers in abundance from the middle of May until late in August—a period of three months. It is to be expected that in the future the hybrids of the autumn-blooming *H. multiflora* will extend the period when good daylilies may be had in flower.

The Amount of Flowers

Many of the best kinds of daylilies yield flowers in abundance. For such varieties there are numerous buds on a scape, and, if a plant has become well-established, scapes to the number of 15 or more are not unusual. The species *H. Middendorffii* and *H. Dumortierii* have few flowers to a scape and the period of bloom is consequently rather short. Tangerine also has few flowers to a scape but the scapes are numerous and the plant possesses distinct value and rare charm. It is possible for the total number of flowers produced by large plants of many varieties to range to several hundred. The number depends on the kind of daylily and on the age and the size of a plant. The period of blooming for a plant usually covers at least three weeks and in the climax of this period a total of twenty-five flowers is not unusual for a single day and as many as 100 are sometimes seen.

In the production of a large number of flowers, daylilies fully compensate for the ephemeral nature of the individual flower. Considering the conspicuous size of the blooms one could scarcely expect plants to yield flowers in greater numbers or to have a more extended period of blooming than do the best of the daylilies.

Fragrance of Daylily Flowers

There is fragrance of pleasing quality from the flowers of certain daylilies. It is strongest or medium in the species *H. flava* and *H. citrina* and in the varieties Lemon Queen, Flava Major, Citronella, Ophir, Aureole, Parthenope, Soudan, Princess, and Yellow Hammer. The odor is weak or moderate in *H. Middendorffii* and *H. Thunbergii,* and for numerous varieties of which mention may be made of Luteola, Shirley, Eldorado, Gold Dust, Apricot, Gold Imperial, Golden Bell, Calypso, Mikado, Wau-Bun, and Vesta. There is no odor, or at least only a faint trace of odor, from flowers of *H. aurantiaca,* of *H. multiflora,* of *H. fulva* (including the clonal strains and numerous wild plants to be classed with this species), of certain varieties such as Margaret Perry and George Yeld, and of many seedlings having *H. fulva* in their parentage.

In a representative collection of daylilies, as they are grown in the flower garden, odor is not an outstanding quality. In its strongest development it is not heavy, lasting, and widely penetrating, but rather delicate and demanding close acquaintance for appreciation.

Form of Flower

The single-flowered class. Most daylilies have "normal" or "single" flowers with six segments in the perianth. But among these there is a wide diversity in the size, the fullness, and the shape of the flowers. Perhaps in time somewhat definite classes may be made according to form and size of flowers but at present these features may be considered largely as individual characteristics and described in such terms as small or large, full or narrow-petaled, trumpet-shaped, bell-shaped, slightly-spreading, spreading, reflexed, and pinched.

The double-flowered class (see plate 7) is represented by the fulvous daylilies cultivated under the names Kwanso, Flore Pleno, and the *H. fulva* Variegated. There is occasional reference to a double-flowered form of *H. flava* but plants received under this name at The New York Botanical Garden have either been single-flowered or have been *H. fulva* clone Kwanso. A double-flowered form of *H. Dumortierii* is mentioned (*Standard Cyclopedia of Horticulture* 3: 1456) but this is evidently an error in statement for there appears to be no such type in existence.

A selection of at least 25 different daylilies must be made if one is to include the best varieties which represent the different garden classes of daylilies. Persons will differ greatly in their judgment and choice of the plants of greatest merit, but most of those varieties and species mentioned in this chapter as good or excellent will meet the approval of the majority of gardeners. Without doubt during the next few years new varieties of special merit will appear in the trade.

Plate 31. Flowers of Vesta Daylily

Plate 32. Flower of Wau-Bun Daylily

Plate 33. Views in a Naturalistic planting of Daylilies in Connecticut Garden

CHAPTER VIII

THE USES OF DAYLILIES

As garden plants daylilies rank among the most valuable of herbaceous perennials. The green foliage comes early in spring, forms a substantial mound, and holds its place attractively throughout the growing season. With many of the best daylilies new leaves continue to appear and the foliage is freshly green until freezing temperatures, and the more nearly evergreen types will remain somewhat green into the winter. For a well-established plant numerous conspicuous flowers open in succession day after day to continue a canopy of color throughout a rather extended period of flowering. A proper selection of species and hybrid clonal varieties will provide areas of color in succession from early May until late August or even into September. To close inspection the individual flower reveals a rare beauty in richness and abundance of color and an exquisite grace in form. In the different species and clonal varieties there is a wide and pleasing diversity in habits of growth, season of flowering, and in the size, shape, and color of the flowers. Daylilies thrive in any soil and in any part of an ordinary garden. Year by year a plant spreads in circumference through the extension of short upright branches, and some daylilies have also spreading rhizomes. The strong and often fleshy roots withstand and defy ordinary drought. Garden weeds do not crowd the daylilies and cannot compete with their compact and sturdy habits of growth. No garden plant is more reliable, more self-sufficient.

In the small garden daylilies are especially valuable when placed in the mixed herbaceous border according to stature and grouped with other plants with consideration to color of flowers and season of flowering. It is to be remembered that the foliage of daylilies, like that of various other perennials (irises, peonies, etc.), is a rather permanent feature of the garden before and after the plants flower. When daylilies are grouped with other plants that bloom at the same time the effect may be enhanced during the period of blooming, but the expanse of green foliage is of course the greater for the rest of the season. The judicious selection and arrangement of certain of the best varieties that provide succession of blooming is perhaps most desired in small gardens, and for this a selection of daylilies now available will provide suitable varieties from May until late August.

In the more extensive gardens daylilies may not only be used liberally in the mixed herbaceous borders but they may be given a prominent place in particular areas or in special gardens. Certain varieties as Tangerine, Estmere, the Lemon Daylily, and Mikado show to advantage as feature plants. Several plants of a variety or of different varieties may be massed to form centers of unusual interest. For a special section devoted to daylilies, clones may be selected which will provide supplementing variety in stature, habits of growth, season of flowering, and color of flowers.

In naturalistic plantings daylilies are particularly effective. The more robust clones are well adapted for naturalistic plantings in such locations as grassy vales, along the banks of streams or lakes, on hilly slopes, and about ledges of rock. Many daylilies flourish in natural competition with grass quite as well as does the Europa Daylily, which is a volunteer escape in the sections where it has long been grown.

The views in plate 33 are of a charming naturalistic planting of daylilies in "Connecticut Garden." This remarkable garden includes several hundred acres devoted to wild and to naturalized plants, and the area has been developed with respect to natural habitats and landscape features according to the plans of the owner, Mr. Benjamin T. Fairchild. A considerable area is devoted to daylilies. Here the summer-flowering *H. Thunbergii* and the *H. fulva* clone Europa are grown in large numbers and during July they provide masses of brilliant color amidst the setting of green in trees and grass. A portion of the area is devoted to early-blooming types, chiefly of *H. flava,* and this part is also rich in color earlier in the season.

As cut flowers. In using the flowers of daylilies for interior decoration consideration should be given to the flowering habits of the different varieties. The purely day-blooming sorts will provide open flowers only during the hours of daylight. Excellent decorative effects may be had with the flowers of any good day-blooming daylily during the hours of daylight. The flowers of daylilies with a longer period of opening than the diurnal will often undergo changes during the evening, especially in the later hours when flowers that have been open may close and buds may open. Thus the aspect of decorations composed of daylilies will change if kept until the second day, and then some attention, rearrangement, and possibly the addition of more flowers from the garden are desirable.

Use of the flowers as food. The flowers of daylilies are extensively used as a food in the Orient and in this use they are regarded as a delicacy especially by the Chinese. In some parts of China daylilies are rather extensively grown as a cultivated crop for the yield of flowers. The flowers may be used fresh from a plant but they are chiefly used in a dried form which is easily handled in commerce and which provides a supply at all times. Packages of one pound and one-half pound sizes are sold very generally in Chinese food shops, even in America, under the names gum-tsoy, meaning golden-vegetable, and gum-jum, meaning golden needles (see plate 34).

In culinary uses the flowers of daylilies are employed chiefly in soups, in various meat dishes, and with noodles. In preparation the basal end of the dried flowers consisting of the ovary is removed and the rest is cut into several segments. Enough water is added to the quantity desired to insure complete soaking and the parts soon become soft, pliable and somewhat gelatinous. In this condition the material is added to soups that are already cooked, and when the whole is brought to a boil again, a matter of a few minutes, the dish is ready to be served. To various dishes of meats and noodles the soaked flowers are added during the final stages of cooking, or the flowers may be cooked separately for a few minutes and added as a garnish—somewhat as mushrooms may be used. To these various dishes the flowers add substance of individual consistency and they supply a distinct and pleasing flavor. Analyses of the commercial product gum-jum show considerable amounts of fat, protein, and carbohydrate and appropriate tests have revealed the presence of vitamins A and B.

The writer has not learned which, if any, type of daylily provides the best flowers for food, or is most widely cultivated in China. The dried flowers in the packages of gum-jum shown in plate 34 appear to be of a type of daylily with narrow perianth-tube, narrow segments, and pale yellow coloring. Living plants obtained from Szechwan through the kindness of Mr. W. P. Hsieh of the University of Chengtu and said to be a type cultivated in that province have flowers of fulvous color and are to be classed as *Hemerocallis fulva.* Probably the flowers of any daylily are suitable for use as food. Flowers of garden plants which are collected as soon as they close may be used but the flavor is somewhat different from that of the dried flowers. A more extended discussion of gum-jum is published in the *Journal of The New York Botanical Garden* (**34**: 97–100. 1933).

CHAPTER IX

CULTURE AND CARE

Planting and transplanting. The most seasonable time for dividing, planting and resetting daylilies is in early spring as soon as it is possible to do the work. But in one's own garden or in moving plants to locations near by, daylilies may be divided and reset or transplanted entire at any time even while they are blooming. If transplanted in summer or early autumn they will become established before the ground is frozen and be ready for prompt growth with the coming of the following spring.

In moving plants it is well to keep considerable earth about the roots, to use such care that the roots are not unnecessarily broken, and to make the transfer promptly. The fibrous and somewhat wiry roots should be spread out radially in a natural position in a hole of ample size rather than rolled into a ball and crowded into a small space.

If plants of daylilies are to be transported a considerable distance they will suffer least if shipped while they are in the dormant condition either in late autumn or in early spring. If plants are received late in autumn or during the winter they may be packed in earth or sand in a cold frame or merely in a box and kept cool, but not too dry, until time for planting in spring. If a greenhouse is available the plants may be kept growing in pots, in flats, or in a bench during the winter. Small divisions of plants are likely to suffer some winter injury if planted directly into the garden late in the autumn.

In general garden culture, it is best to allow plants of daylilies to remain undisturbed until they become well established. For a few years there will be some increase in the height of the plant and, what is more gratifying, there will be an increase in the number of scapes and flowers. After a period of a number of years of uninterrupted growth and spread, the numerous branches of a plant become crowded in the central portion and the crown may become somewhat elevated, and then the plant should be divided and replanted.

Soils and locations. The soil of any ordinary garden is suitable for daylilies. In naturalistic plantings they will thrive in pockets of soil along ledges of rock, in rather dry areas, or in moist soil along brooks or ponds. They develop best in sunny exposures. In the shade and also in rich soil, they are likely to be lush and rank with the scapes somewhat tall, slender, and weak.

Care in the garden. Aside from proper planting and transplanting daylilies require almost no attention. In the garden and in the herbaceous border one will merely till the soil about the plants to destroy weeds and to maintain a tidy appearance. The flower stalks should be removed soon after the plants are through blooming and the older leaves may be removed as they die in late summer. For many daylilies a vigorous growth of new and attractive foliage develops in late summer and autumn. During the winter the cluster of dead leaves functions as a protecting mulch to the crown. In the spring the dead leaves may be removed. The more robust types in naturalistic plantings need merely to be left alone except, perhaps, for the removal of scapes and of dead leaves.

Insect pests and diseases of a serious or even troublesome nature have never been reported for daylilies. During the several years of rather extensive culture of daylilies at The New York Botanical Garden there have been only minor and transitory attacks of either insects or fungi. Certain leaf-spot fungi have occasionally been observed late in summer on leaves that are still green. In a few cases plants have been attacked by thrips which feed on the tissues in the base of leaves causing the foliage to die prematurely. As a means of precaution plants which showed considerable infestation have been dug and destroyed. But if such a plant was rare the leaves were removed and burned. Plants thus treated were usually vigorous and fully healthy in the following year.

The experience with daylilies wherever they are grown seems to indicate that they possess a freedom from diseases and insect pests that is surpassed by no other garden plant. Fortunately they have none of the virus diseases that are very destructive of their sister plants, the members of the genus *Lilium*.

Winter injury. In the northern part of United States and farther north daylilies which have the evergreen habit of growth usually suffer to some extent from winter injury. The more active foliage buds continue to send forth the tips of young leaves during the autumn and these remain lush and green for some time after freezing temperatures occur. In the region about New York there is usually a protection of snow for only a small part of the winter and there is an alternation of freezing and thawing temperatures. When spring arrives many of the exposed leaves have been killed and some buds may be dead. For a time the upper portion of such plants is in poor condition in comparison with the appearance of the fully hardy types which start growth early in spring from dormant buds. But in most varieties, the buds which are still alive and the more undeveloped buds in the crown soon put forth new leaves and make a good plant which flowers freely. Many of the summer-blooming sorts that have the *H. aurantiaca* or the *H. aurantiaca* clone Major as a parent are of this class. Of these mention may be made of Aureole, Ajax, Wau-Bun, Mikado, Cinnabar, Luteola, and Sir Michael Foster.

The *H. aurantiaca* clone Major suffers so severely from winter injury that it usually does not survive the winters throughout most of northern United States. Many seedlings obtained by hybridizing *H. aurantiaca* and *H. aurantiaca* clone Major with more hardy daylilies are not fully hardy.

A cover of coarse hay, straw, or evergreen boughs will provide some protection to the evergreen types and will lessen the extent of injury to them during winter. By such means the *H. aurantiaca* Major has been kept alive from year to year in the experimental garden at The New York Botanical Garden.

The dwarf or semi-dwarf species *H. Forrestii, H. nana,* and *H. plicata* grow poorly both in England and in northern United States. But whether this is due to tenderness or to unfavorable conditions of soil or culture is not, at the present time, fully apparent.

In semi-tropical and tropical countries certain daylilies are being grown with success. In the southern states the types and varieties which are evergreen, or nearly so, are said to be most satisfactory. Of these *H. fulva, H. aurantiaca, H. aurantiaca* clone Major, Aureole, Semperflorens, Ajax, Luteola, Sir Michael Foster, and Mikado may be mentioned. The species and hybrid clones whose foliage becomes fully dormant in the winter grow somewhat poorly in the tropics and in various localities do not survive. This class includes especially *H. minor, H. Dumortierii, H. Middendorffii,* Orangeman, Apricot, Estmere, and Gold Dust.

The culture of daylilies in Florida has been studied especially by Professor H. Harold Hume, Assistant Director of Research, Agricultural Experiment Station of the University of Florida, who has prepared for this volume the following statement.

"In Florida, where but few of the more common perennials used in other parts of the country are satisfactory, the daylilies are a welcome addition to the lists of garden plants. This is more particularly true because of the ease with which they may be grown and their adaptability to a wide range of soil and exposure conditions. They may be found here and there in gardens from the northern boundary down into the southern portions of the state, everywhere apparently at home—in sun and shade on many different types of soil.

"Of the two groups into which daylilies may be divided, deciduous and evergreen, the latter are, on the whole, more widely adapted and satisfactory. When not in flower the plants are still good green masses and evergreen plants in the garden are commonly more highly prized. The deciduous sorts are satisfactory in the northern portion of the state and as they bloom early they are of value in lengthening the flowering season. Far south their winter rest period is not so prolonged or definite and in consequence they do not appear to behave satisfactorily. Conclusions as to whether they will be satisfactory or not in a given locality should not be reached too hastily. The plants should be given at least two seasons in which to become established, with their roots well down into the soil, before an opinion is passed upon their value. It often happens on first blooming that the flowers are borne low down among the foliage on very short scapes, but in another season the stems grow out to normal length.

"With a given assortment of varieties, daylilies are in flower from March through August in the northern part of the state, the earliest to bloom being the deciduous group represented by such varieties as Apricot, Gold Dust, Orangeman and Sovereign. Blooming about the same time are two other taller, larger-flowered sorts, Aureole and Queen of May. The season of most abundant bloom comes during May and June. This is the season for such varieties as Mikado, Vesta, Margaret Perry, Kwanso, Gypsy, Mrs. A. H. Austin, The Gem, Modesty and Florham. Later in coming into flower are Cressida, Cinnabar and *H. aurantiaca* clone Major. These, together with some of the later midseason sorts, serve to extend the blooming season.

"Any time of the year is planting time in Florida for daylilies, though the season November through March should be given preference. If good plants are set then, flowers may be expected within a few weeks, but if small and weak they are not likely to bloom until another season. Goodly preparation of the soil with the addition of peat or leaf mold is advisable and applications of commercial fertilizer, containing 4 per cent ammonia, 8 per cent phosphoric acid and 4 per cent potash, for instance, and of well rotted dairy fertilizer, are desirable. Watering during the season of active growth should be liberal especially on well-drained lands. In selecting a location, it is well to choose one for the lighter colored, thinner petaled varieties, like Modesty and *H. Thunbergii,* that will afford some shade, as their flowers are likely to bleach or burn out during hot, dry weather."

This statement will, no doubt, apply equally well to a large portion of the subtropical and tropical areas of the world.

The culture of daylilies involves no special difficulties and there are probably few if any localities throughout the world where flower gardens are maintained in which at least some of the daylilies may not be grown successfully. Evidently the various kinds of daylilies may be grown in a wide belt of latitude in each of the Temperate zones. Presumably the more nearly evergreen types are most suitable for culture in tropical areas.

CHAPTER X

PROPAGATION, SEED REPRODUCTION, AND BREEDING

Vegetative Propagation

Division. Daylilies are easily propagated by the simple and effective method of dividing the plants. For successful propagation a plant may be divided into small sections, providing each one comprises a piece of the crown with at least one bud and a few roots. These may be placed directly in the garden or kept for a time in pots. So tenaceous of life are daylilies that an uprooted plant or a segment of a plant which is left lying on the ground will live and grow for some time and may even take root in the soil and become established.

The Lemon Daylily (*H. flava*) and the various clones of fulvous daylilies (Europa, Maculata, Cypriana, and Kwanso) have sturdy creeping rhizomes (see plate 35) that may extend through the soil to a distance of a foot or more before they turn upward to produce roots and leaves. These young plants at the ends of the rhizomes may be removed for planting, especially after they have had time to develop fleshy roots and a few crown branches. If left alone they extend the area occupied by the plant. Some of the clonal varieties obtained by cross-breeding with *H. flava* or with the clones of *H. fulva* also have widely spreading rootstocks.

But most species and many of the named clones of daylilies have a compact habit of stem growth beneath the soil (plate 36). The branches in the crown of the plant spread on all sides but they ascend almost directly and hence the plants spread more slowly and more compactly than do plants of *H. flava* and *H. fulva.* Such plants may, however, be divided or broken up into segments for propagation.

In nursery practice the effort should be made to produce strong plants well supplied with fleshy roots and growing buds so that vigorous growth will continue after the transplanting and a good showing of flowers will soon be made. To develop such plants to best advantage there should be rather frequent division of the nursery stock so that no plant becomes unduly large and compact. This treatment will yield better individuals for transplanting than are to be obtained when old compact plants are broken up into pieces. A plant with three to four buds is worth more for planting than a smaller segment with only one bud, and a plant with five to six buds in the crown is still more desirable. Possibly nurserymen will be willing to offer for sale plants of different sizes with the prices graded in proportion.

Proliferations. When proliferations develop on the flower scapes they may be used in propagation. These somewhat anomalous structures arise as buds and develop into small plants with stem and leaves, and frequently with roots also. They may develop to the condition when they merely sit upon the scape with only a slight attachment to it, but sometimes they remain firmly attached to the scape as a branch. After the blooming period is past and shortly before the scapes have died, the proliferations may be broken off or cut out together with a section of the scape and then handled as cuttings. With reasonable care these little plants develop rapidly to a size suitable for planting in the garden. Many sorts of daylilies never have proliferations, but various hybrids and polyploids have them rather abundantly, in which case they may be utilized if a plant is rare and rapid propagation is desired.

Seed Reproduction in Daylilies

Seeds make possible a more rapid multiplication than does vegetative propagation. Thus a single plant of the Lemon Daylily may yield several hundred seeds from which fine plants may be had in the course of two or three years. It will require some care and labor to rear the seedlings but this effort may be justified and amply repaid if a large number of plants must be quickly obtained.

Few daylilies reproduce true to type by seed. Even the seedlings of the cultivated clones of such species as the Lemon Daylily and Thunberg's Daylily are mostly inferior to the parent clones especially in the size and the fullness of the flowers. Most daylilies such as Apricot, Sovereign, Luteola, Tangerine, Mikado, etc., are hybrids and in some cases are complex hybrids with more than two species involved in the ancestry. Such plants cannot be expected to breed true to type when their seeds are used for reproduction. Also many daylilies do not set seed to their own pollen due to the conditions of self-incompatibility in fertilization and for such plants the seeds produced in the garden are the result of cross-pollinations and are certain to give hybrids more or less different from the seed parents. Thus for nearly all daylilies grown in gardens the seeds cannot be used to reproduce the same type.

Breeding daylilies. The chief value of the seeds of daylilies is in the opportunity they afford for the development of new types through hybridization and selective breeding. Some of the hybrids of garden origin were seedlings probably of incidental pollination by insects. More recently the breeding has been deliberate; the parents have been selected and the pollinations controlled. Hybrids of merit thus obtained are then propagated by division to give clones. In growing seedlings of most daylilies the large proportion will be worthless or of little value, or at least not superior to the best of the named varieties already in the trade. The author has critically selected parents and continued selective breeding for as many as five generations to obtain types, such as the Theron Daylily, that are new and of special merit. In this breeding effort about 15,000 seedlings have already been grown; but thus far only fourteen seedlings have been named for culture in gardens. About 100 seedlings of special merit are being used in selective breeding and some of them are being considered for introduction to the trade.

The possibilities for further improvement of daylilies may, to some degree, be suggested by the mention of some of the aims in the author's work with these plants. In respect to the colors of flowers, selective breeding is in progress in the efforts to develop (1) white flowers, (2) pink and red flowers of sprightly shades, (3) eyed or banded patterns in bold but pleasing colors, and (4) strongly bicolored patterns. The species *H. multiflora* has as many as seventy-five to one hundred buds to a scape and hence its use in hybridization may greatly increase the number of flowers in new varieties beyond that of any of the varieties of today. The double-flowered types now in existence may prove valuable in the development of new double-flowered types that are highly pleasing in appearance. Possibly the lasting quality of the flowers may be extended or prolonged in which case the term "daylily" would become a misnomer. The origin of new forms of flowers is possible. Seedlings with flowers that have petals somewhat frilled or fluted have appeared which indicates that further variations in this particular and in other features of form may be expected. There is chance for some extension in the size of flowers, for lengthening the season of bloom for the group of daylilies, for the production of more and better dwarf forms, for the development of giant types, and for increasing the number of varieties that have stiffly erect, dark green and evergreen foliage.

When one considers the possibilities for the improvement of daylilies it can truly be said that selective breeding in this group of plants has scarcely begun.

Sterilities in Daylilies. The breeding of daylilies is decidedly limited by sterilities that operate to reduce and even entirely to prevent seed setting. One is not able to obtain the seeds of many daylilies by self-pollinations, and many crosses which one may wish to make will not yield seeds. The breeding of daylilies has been much retarded and delayed because the behavior of their sterilities was not understood.

In breeding daylilies one encounters four main types of sterility:

(1) There appears to be lack of affinity between certain species

in the relations of fertilization. Yet hybrids have been obtained from many of the inter-specific combinations.

(2) There is much abortion of spores in (a) certain hybrids, as of *H. flava* × *H. nana*, and (b) in triploids, as the Europa Daylily. This condition greatly reduces the chance that a plant will bear seeds but there may be a few viable pollen grains in which case the plant may be used as a pollen parent.

(3) There is abortion of pistils in the older double-flowered forms, which it happens are also triploid. But in these there is some viable pollen.

(4) In daylilies there are many cases of incompatibility in fertilization which limit or prevent seed to self-pollination, to intraclonal pollination and to certain cross-pollinations between sister seedlings. Studies have been made which reveal that in such cases the pollen tubes grow poorly in the style or fail to function at the ovary chamber or within it. There is a physiological incompatibility in the processes of fertilization. There may be complete self-incompatibility, as in the Europa Daylily. There may be feeble self-compatibility, as in the common garden clone of *H. Thunbergii*, in which case a few seeds may be obtained to selfing. Sometimes an individual or a clone, as the *H. flava* shown in plates 1 and 2, is highly self-fruitful. The same range of results are to be obtained in the cross-relations between sister seedlings and less closely related seedlings or clones. While incompatibilities are hereditary and especially operative within a species or variety, it is possible that they are also involved in the relations between species.

Methods of breeding. The flowers of daylilies are large and the stamens and pistils are conspicuous. In self-pollination the pollen of dehisced stamens is placed on the stigmatic end of the pistil of the same flower. In cross-breeding the pollen of a desired pollen parent is used. If one wishes to be certain of the parentage the pollinations should be controlled. Flower buds may be enclosed in paper bags during the afternoon at which time those intended for crosses may be opened and the anthers removed. Flowers that are diurnal may be pollinated during the forenoon; those that are nocturnal may be worked during the evening. The flowers that are pollinated should be labelled with tags that are marked for identification and appropriate records kept. Bags of "glassine" paper are almost transparent and allow enclosed flowers to develop more normally than do bags of opaque paper.

In daylilies the efforts in hybridization involve making proper specific-pollinations. Further breeding of hybrids, and especially selective breeding, depends largely on finding the relations that are able to produce seeds.

Rearing seedlings. The method of rearing seedlings of daylilies employed by the writer with signal success is as follows. As soon as the seeds are ripe they are planted in seed pans. Usually there is prompt germination. The seedlings are placed in flats or in small pots and kept in a greenhouse during the first winter of their growth. As they increase in size they are transplanted to larger pots according to their needs. For a time in early spring the seedlings are placed in a cold frame. Usually by late spring the seedlings of many types become lusty plants whose roots often fill four-inch or even six-inch pots and then they are planted in rows or beds in the nursery. With such treatment some seedlings produce flowers during the first summer of their growth. But the young seedlings of certain types, as *H. Middendorffii*, *H. minor*, and *H. Dumortierii*, are dormant during the winter when grown in a greenhouse and may require at least two years to reach blooming size. Various progenies of hybrid origin having *H. aurantiaca*, *H. aurantiaca* clone Major, and various types of *H. fulva* in the parentage are not fully hardy and suffer severely or are killed during a winter such as occurs about New York City.

In case greenhouse facilities are not available, the seeds of daylilies may be planted in the spring either in flats that are kept in cold frames or directly in special seed beds in the garden. At least one transplanting may be needed to give the seedlings proper room but they will scarcely be large enough the first summer for planting in rows in a nursery and they may require some protection during the first winter of their growth.

The first flowers produced by a seedling plant will give some indication of their color, size, and form and will usually allow one to form judgment regarding the seedlings that are of no special merit and which may be discarded. But the precise character of the flowers, the habit of growth, and especially the more mature stature of a plant are best determined after several years of development.

APPENDIX A

KEY TO ABBREVIATIONS OF PUBLICATIONS CITED FREQUENTLY IN THE TEXT

This list has been adapted from Appendix I of the original edition of A. B. Stout's *Daylilies* and the notes are his. The bibliographical information has not been updated.

Addisonia. *Addisonia*. Journal with colored plates and descriptions of plants. Published by the New York Botanical Garden. Number 2 of volume 14 and number 1 of volume 15 are devoted entirely to daylilies and include sixteen colored plates.

Bot. Mag. *Curtis's Botanical Magazine*. Established in 1786. Now published for the Royal Horticultural Society, London.

Cir. 42. *The Yellow Daylilies*, by B. Y. Morrison. U. S. Department of Agriculture, Circular 42. Washington, D. C., 1928.

Gard. *The Garden*. An illustrated weekly journal of horticulture. Published in London from 1872 until December 1927.

Gard. Chr. *Gardeners' Chronicle*. Weekly, published in London. For many years this publication has contained articles of importance on daylilies.

Gen. Herbarum. *Gentes Herbarum*. Published by Dr. L. H. Bailey at Ithaca, New York. Fascicle III of volume 2 is devoted to *Hosta* (the plantain lilies) and to the species of *Hemerocallis*.

Hort. *Horticulture*. Published semimonthly at Boston. The official publication of the Massachusetts Horticultural Society, the Horticultural Society of New York, and the Pennsylvania Horticultural Society.

House and Garden. *House and Garden*. Published in New York. Several articles by the author, some of which gave first mention of new clonal varieties of daylilies, have appeared in this periodical [see Appendix B].

Jour. N.Y. Bot. Gard. *Journal of the New York Botanical Garden*. Published monthly. Various articles by the author dealing with daylilies have appeared in the journal [see Appendix B].

Jour. Roy. Hort. Soc. *Journal and Proceedings of the Royal Horticultural Society*, London.

Notes Bot. Gard. Edinburgh. *Notes from the Royal Botanic Garden, Edinburgh*. Glasgow, H. M. Stationery Office.

Rep. Third Conf. Genetics. *Report of the Third International Conference on Genetics, London, 1906*. Published by the Royal Horticultural Society, London, 1907.

Rev. Hort. *Revue Horticole*. Founded in 1829. Published in Paris.

Standard Cyclopedia of Horticulture. *Standard Cyclopedia of Horticulture*, compiled and edited by L. H. Bailey, 3 v. New York, Macmillan, 1928. Contains a synopsis of the genus *Hemerocallis* with mention of various of the older hybrids and so-called varieties.

APPENDIX B

PUBLICATIONS ON HEMEROCALLIS BY A. B. STOUT AND HIS COLLEAGUES

The following is a chronological record compiled by A. B. Stout in 1949 listing his publications on *Hemerocallis*, with comments which indicate the progress to that time of the research that had been done on this genus at the New York Botanical Garden.

1919

1. Seed Sterility in Plants that Reproduce Vegetatively. *Journal of the New York Botanical Garden* 20:104-5.

   This is a report of studies on the sterility and fertility of the few types of daylilies that were then at the New York Botanical Garden. Capsules and seeds had been obtained of *Hemerocallis flava* and by the hybridizations of *H. flava* and *H. thunbergii* x *H. fulva* clone Europa.

1921

2. Sterility and Fertility in Hemerocallis. *Torreya* 21:57-62.

   A report of further hybridizations which included plants of *Hemerocallis minor* and *H. aurantiaca*. A photograph was shown of capsules and seeds of the Europa daylily x *H. thunbergii*.

1925

3. New Daylilies. *Journal of the New York Botanical Garden* 26:169-78.

   A report on progress on the assembly of species and cultivated clones and on the breeding work. There were about 1,500 seedlings of which nearly half had either the Europa Daylily or *Hemerocallis aurantiaca* in the ancestry. At this time the collection of living plants included members of nearly all the known species and the named horticultural clones, and some plants had been received from China and Japan. There were three illustrations showing a group of hybrids of clone Luteola x *H. aurantiaca* and also flowers of seedlings some of which were of large size or dark red in coloring. There was a wide range of color variations from light yellow to dark orange and in the red colors there were extremes of both reduction and intensification. The color patterns included bicolors and the midzone pattern of the Mikado clone type.

1926

4. The Capsules, Seeds, and Seedlings of the Orange Daylily. *Journal of Heredity* 17:243-49.

This summarizes the experimental studies on the sterility and fertility of the clone Europa. Twenty-three capsules had been obtained of 7,135 cross-pollinated flowers; about 1,200 seedlings had Europa in their ancestry. Plants of the clones Maculata and Cypriana and also wild plants of fulvous daylilies had been obtained and used in breeding. A summary was made of the seedlings grown by George Yeld and Amos Perry in England. Mention was made of the first letter received by the writer from C. Betscher that was written after Betscher had seen the 1925 publication noted above.

1927

5. Studies of the Inheritance of Self- and Cross-Incompatibility. *Memoirs of the Horticultural Society of New York* 3:345-52.

Given here is tabulated data on the fertility and incompatibility in all self- and cross-relations for twelve hybrids of *Hemerocallis thunbergii* x *H. aurantiaca.* Eight of the plants were self-incompatible and four were self-fertile to some degree. There were many cross-incompatibilities and reciprocal differences.

1929

6. The Fulvous Daylilies, I. *Journal of the New York Botanical Garden* 30:129-36.

The name Europa was applied for the first time to the widely cultivated clone which is the historical type that Linnaeus (1762) named *Hemerocallis fulva*. Descriptions and the histories of the two double-flowered clones Flore Pleno and Kwanso were given with photographs of the flowers.

It may be stated here that there has been much error in horticultural literature regarding these double-flowered clones. New names have been given to them; the name Virginica was applied to Flore Pleno. Ramets of them have been called new seedlings and even introduced as such. The writer has answered numerous letters of inquiry concerning the identity, character, and history of these clones. The facts regarding these matters are fully recorded in botanical and horticultural literature.

7. The Fulvous Daylilies, II. *Journal of the New York Botanical Garden* 30:185-94.

This was a report on the fulvous daylilies (1) described in botanical literature, (2) in cultivation in Europe, and (3) received at the New York Botanical Garden from China and Japan. A photograph was reproduced showing a flower of each of four wild fulvous daylilies, one of which was the pink-flowered plant that was propagated and later named Rosalind. It was reported that the fulvous daylilies closely related to *Hemerocallis fulva* clone Europa are a variable group in respect to form and color of the flowers and that certain of them are "certain to be of value in culture and in the breeding of new horticultural types."

8. Chromosome Irregularities in Relation to Sterility in *Hemerocallis fulva* clone Europa. *Annals of the New York Academy of Science* 31: 1-30.

This paper was a collaboration with Torasaburo Susa, who assisted in the cytological studies for one year. Earlier studies had described many irregularities in the sporogenesis of plants of "*Hemerocallis fulva.*" Estimates of 24, 32, 33, and 48 had been made for the somatic number of chromosomes in the plants. In the preparations made by Susa there were somatic numbers of 12, 20, 26, and 30. There were extreme differences in the numbers which spores received. It was considered that members of the clone Europa were polyploid for a basic genome number of 12. But it was later decided that the clone is a triploid with a basic number of 11 chromosomes and that this is the basic genome number in all the species of the genus that have been studied.

9. New Daylilies for the Garden. *House and Garden* 55 (January):88-89.

This article provides the descriptions for the first of the named clones of *Hemerocallis* that were developed at the New York Botanical Garden. These clones are (1) Mikado, (2) Vesta, and (3) Wau-Bun. There were reports on the parentage. The following statement was made: "The New York Botanical Garden cannot undertake the propagation of these new daylilies for general distribution or sale. It happens that for several years preceding his death, Mr. Bertrand H. Farr exhibited keen interest in this breeding work and assisted it by obtaining and contributing plants of several species and varieties. The firm which succeeded to his business has continued this helpful cooperation."

10. The Charms of the Modern Daylilies. *House and Garden* 55 (May):118-19.

    This was an evaluation of the garden values of daylilies with illustrations of several of the new clones.

11. Descriptions and colored plates in *Addisonia* 14.

    Plate 457, *Hemerocallis flava*; 458, *H. minor*; 459, *H. thunbergii*; 460, *H. fulva* clone Maculata; 461, *H. aurantiaca*; 462, *H. dumortierii*; 463, *H. middendorffii*; 464, *H. multiflora* Stout sp. nov.

1930

12. Daylilies for Your Garden. *Ladies Home Journal*, February.

    This a popular discussion of the species, clones, and new hybrids of daylilies and of their uses and values as garden subjects. There are twelve reproductions of colored photographs, and previous to this date few reproductions of this type had been made. One photograph shows flowers of two unnamed seedlings that had orange-red and dark red coloring in the flowers.

13. Botanical Observations in Europe. *Journal of the New York Botanical Garden* 31:261-64.

    Special attention was given to daylilies during a trip to France, Italy, Germany, and England. Visits were made to Vilmorin-Andrieux et Cie. near Paris, to Willy Müller and his garden in Naples, and to the Royal Botanical Garden in Munich. A day was spent with Mr. George Yeld and another with Mr. Amos Perry in England. The very complete collections of daylilies maintained at Wisley, England by the Royal Horticultural Society and at the Royal Botanical Gardens at Kew were studied. The living plants upon which the original descriptions of *Hemerocallis thunbergii*, *H. aurantiaca*, and *H. aurantiaca* clone Major were based had been kept and propagated at Kew. These were seen and ramets of each were obtained and grown at the New York Botanical Garden. All of the herbarium specimens of *Hemerocallis* at Kew were evaluated.

14. Descriptions and colored plates of *Hemerocallis* in *Addisonia* 15.

Plate 481, *Hemerocallis forrestii*. The flower shown was from the first plant bearing this species name that came to the New York Botanical Garden from the Royal Botanical Gardens at Kew, England. It may now be stated that this plant was not a member of the species *H. forrestii*. The unbranched character of the flower scape was like that of certain hybrids that had *H. nana* for a parent. 482, *H. citrina*; 483, *H. fulva longituba*; 484, *H. fulva* L. var. *rosea* Stout, var. nov.; 485, clone Luteola; 486, clone Gold Dust; 487, clone Mikado; and 488, clone Wau-Bun.

15. The New Species *Hemerocallis multiflora*. *Journal of the New York Botanical Garden* 31:34-39.

An account of the introduction of the first plants of this type, of their character and variation in habits of growth, and of the extent to which they had been used in hybridizations. There were reproductions of four photographs that showed plants, scapes, and flowers.

1931

16. Notes on New Hybrid Daylilies. *Journal of the New York Botanical Garden* 32:25-33.

The first description of Cinnabar. It was reported that the collection of species and horticultural clones included representatives of most of the known daylilies.

17. The Landscape Values of Daylilies. *Arts and Decoration*, March.

A popular survey of the diversity, character, and values of daylilies, with ten illustrations.

18. Pollen-tube Behavior in Self-incompatibility. *Report of the Proceedings of the Fifth International Botanical Congress, Cambridge, England, 1930*. Cambridge: Cambridge University Press, 255-56.

1932

19. The Bijou Daylily; of a New Small-Flowered Race. *Journal of the New York Botanical Garden* 33:1-4.

The Bijou Daylily was the first seedling to be named that had *Hemerocallis multiflora* in its parentage. Photographs of a plant and of flowers were reproduced.

20. The Soudan Daylily. *Journal of the New York Botanical Garden* 33:104-5.

The first description and illustration of the Soudan Daylily.

21. Chromosome Numbers in Hemerocallis with Reference to Triploidy and Secondary Polyploidy. *Cytologia* 3:250-59.

Cytological studies show that a somatic diploid number of 22 chromosomes is the rule for species of *Hemerocallis*, that triploidy exists in several cultivated clones of *H. fulva*, and that diploids, triploids, and aneuploids with somatic numbers from 20 to 28 were found among the progenies of triploids crossed with diploids. There were variations in the somatic cells of individual plants. No tetraploids were obtained. The clones Europa, Maculata, Flore Pleno, and Kwanso are triploid.

1933

22. Gum-jum and Gum-tsoy: a Food from the Flowers of Daylilies. *Journal of the New York Botanical Garden* 34:97-100.

An account of the commercial preparation of the flowers of daylilies for use as food with a photograph of packages of dried flowers.

23. A Display Garden of Daylilies. *Journal of the New York Botanical Garden* 34:135-39.

This presents a diagram of the first special display garden for daylilies that was constructed at the New York Botanical Garden. There is a list of the species, horticultural clones, and hybrids that were represented and of the persons, nursery firms, botanical gardens, and sources in the Orient from which plants had been obtained.

24. *Hemerocallis aurantiaca* and *Hemerocallis aurantiaca* Major. *The New Flora and Silva* 5:187-92.

This gives the history, origin, and description of each of these daylilies with a photograph of the flowers. Both have evergreen foliage but the two are distinct in the size and color of the flowers. Both are clones of uncertain botanical status. The application of the scientific specific names to these is certainly a taxonomic error. At the time of the present writing, it may be stated that the so-called *Hemerocallis aurantiaca* has the breeding behavior of a hybrid and that the so-called *H. aurantiaca* clone Major may be a member of a distinct orange-flowered race or even wild species that will be recognized when the wild daylilies of southern China are critically studied. The clone that Hans Sass called *H. aurantiaca* Major is distinctly different from the true clone of this name which has been grown at Kew and elsewhere since the time of its first description.

25. Pollen-tube Behavior in Hemerocallis with Special Reference to Incompatibilities. *Bulletin of the Torrey Botanical Club* 60:397-416.

Dr. Clyde Chandler, who was technical assistant to the writer from 1927 until 1943, was a joint author of this paper. The long pistils of *Hemerocallis* flowers have a stylar canal on the wall of which pollen tubes travel. The reactions of incompatibility in daylilies may be complete in the upper part of the style, or near the entrance to the ovary, or few or no seeds may be formed when pollen tubes enter the ovary. A plate of illustration shows the structure of the pistils and there are figures showing curves of pollen-tube growth. The feeble self-fertility in a plant of *H. thunbergii*, which is a condition common in daylilies, was analyzed.

26. The Daylily Taruga. *Horticulture*, January.

The first description and illustration of this clone.

27. The Flowering Habits of Daylilies. *Journal of the New York Botanical Garden* 34:25-32.

Descriptions and illustrations are given of the three main types of anthesis in daylilies: the diurnal; the nocturnal; and the extended. The overlap of old and new sets is illustrated in flowers of the Lemon Daylily and in flowers of the hybrid clone of Gold Dust. Drawings of the latter were published in the first *Yearbook of the Midwest Hemerocallis Society* (1947) without mention of the fact that there had been previous publication and discussion.

1934

28. *Hemerocallis exaltata* Stout, sp. nov. *Addisonia* 18.

Plate 595 is a colored plate showing a flower, a capsule, a seed, and the upper portion of a scape. It is accompanied by a description and a statement of the origin of the type plants.

29. Hemerocallis Theron. *The Gardeners' Chronicle*, January.

A description of this clone with a record of parentage and an illustration of a flower.

30. Dwarf Daylilies. *Journal of the New York Botanical Garden* 35:1-8.

Discussion and illustrations of *Hemerocallis nana*, *H. plicata*, *H. forrestii*, *H. fulva angustifolia*, a dwarf clone somewhat resembling

H. dumortierii, *H. minor*, and various horticultural clones incorrectly called dwarf. A first mention was made of seventy-four hybrid seedlings of *H. flava* x *H. nana*. It may now be stated that these were interesting hybrids but that none will be introduced for garden culture. A seedling that was named Nada in this article later increased in stature until it was no longer dwarf and then it was discarded.

31. Better and Newer Daylilies for All. *House and Garden*, March.

A description and list of some of the best clones of daylilies available to gardeners.

32. *Daylilies; The Wild Species and Garden Clones, Both Old and New, of the Genus Hemerocallis*. New York: The Macmillan Company.

This is a volume of 119 pages and thirty-six plates of which four that are colored were previously published in *Addisonia*. Various of the uncolored illustrations had also been published earlier. [The four "colored" illustrations, nos. 1, 6, 11, and 20, are here reproduced in black and white. New color plates have been added.] There are ten chapters, an appendix, and an index. There is a list of the horticultural clones then known to the author, and five new clones were mentioned for the first time: Charmaine, Jubilee, Majestic, Princess, and Vulcan.

33. Distribution of Seedling Daylilies. *Journal of the New York Botanical Garden* 35:189.

In response to notices sent to all members of the New York Botanical Garden during July 1934, about 150 members received ten each of the best of the seedlings that were being discarded that summer.

Between 1920 and 1936, a total of at least five thousand of the best seedlings of some fifty thousand discards were distributed to garden members, and especially to some who had contributed to the support of the botanical gardens. It was soon learned that some of these plants were obtained by nurserymen and by breeders and in some cases were sold as named clones. In one instance, seeds of narrow-petalled and red-flowered plants of these discards were advertised and sold at ten cents each and divisions were sold for as much as nine dollars. After 1936, no distributions of discarded seedlings were made.

It may now be stated that divisions of *Hemerocallis fulva rosea* clone Rosalind and plants and seeds of *H. multiflora* were widely distributed to botanical gardens, to gardeners, and to plant breeders, including Amos Perry in England and Mrs. Thomas Nesmith in the United States. More than twenty-five persons received a division of the clone Rosalind before it was given this clonal name. Divisions of species and named clones were also given to numerous public gardens for display, but after 1930 most of such contributions were made directly from the Farr Nursery Company.

1935

34. The Lemon Daylily (*Hemerocallis flava* L.): Its Origin and Status. *Journal of the New York Botanical Garden* 36:61-68.

The Lemon Daylily was in cultivation in France and Belgium in 1570. It has been propagated as a clone and widely distributed. There are several clones, as "*flava major*," that are evidently hybrids. Seedlings grown from the selfed seeds of the Lemon Daylily are variable in the size and shape of flowers, and none has been hardy at New York. Presumably this plant originated in the Orient or arose from plants that came from there. "There is no reliable evidence that a wild type or species which has the essential botanical characters of this plant now exists in the Orient." It may now be stated for the record that the writer has examined numerous herbarium specimens of collections in the Orient including those that were labelled "*Hemerocallis flava*." In no case does such a plant have the peculiar semifasciated scape that is characteristic of the clone that bears the name *H. flava*. At the present time one cannot make a satisfactory statement regarding the origin of this old familiar garden clone. It is, however, distinct from any of the other types of *Hemerocallis* that have been described as species.

35. New Developments in Daylilies. *Journal of the New York Botanical Garden* 36:205-16.

In part this is the publication of a radio talk. In addition, there is a report on the main aims of the research on daylilies, a statement of the progress of this work, an explanation of the distributions of the new clones by the Farr Nursery Company, and a description, with illustrations, of the new clones Bagdad, Chengtu, Dauntless, Midas, Patricia, Rajah, Serenade, Summer Multiflora Hybrids, and Sonny.

36. The Daylily on the Cover. *Horticulture* 13(September 1):394.

A history and a description of the Chengtu Daylily, with a group of three flowers reproduced on the cover in almost natural size.

37. Developments in Daylilies. *Gardeners' Chronicle of America*, September:259-60.
38. Daylilies for Southern Gardens. *Garden Gateways*, April.
39. The Species of Daylilies. *Yearbook; American Amaryllis Society* 1935:98-100.

1936

40. New Daylilies. *Herbertia* 3:92-95, 113.
    First descriptions with illustrations of the clones Linda and Wolof.
41. The Horticultural Clones of Daylilies and Their Evaluation. *Herbertia* 3:99-103.
42. Some Results of Selective Breeding with Hemerocallis. *Records of the Genetics Society of America*.
    An abstract of a report on the genetical aspects of developments in intensified coloring.
43. Bicolored Daylilies. *House and Garden* 69(June):61.
44. Daylilies—From Field to Fame. *House Beautiful* 78(May):64-65.
45. Daylilies. Norman Taylor, ed. *The Garden Dictionary*. Boston: Houghton Mifflin.

1937

46. Vegetative Propagation of Daylilies. *Journal of the New York Botanical Garden* 38:13-17.
    Discussion with illustrations of section cuttings and of natural proliferations.
47. Two New Daylilies. *Journal of the New York Botanical Garden* 38:60.
    Descriptions of the Saturn and Circe daylilies.
48. The Horticultural Status of Daylilies. *Herbertia* 4:130-36.
49. A List of the New Clones of Daylilies. *Herbertia* 4:144-60.
    A list of 104 clones introduced since 1934.
50. Daylilies. *Horticultural News* (Michigan Horticultural Society) 4, no. 1.
51. Diversity in Daylilies. *Handbook; International Flower Show of 1937*.
    A report, with photograph, of the display garden of *Hemerocallis* at the New York Botanical Garden and suggestions on the selection of twenty-five of the best clones.

52. The Public Display Garden of Daylilies. *Journal of the New York Botanical Garden* 38:147-49.

A description, with a photograph, of the new display collection of daylilies.

1938

53. Daylilies with Rosy Pink Coloring. *Horticulture* 16(May 15):226.

This article explains the status of the botanical variety *Hemerocallis fulva* var. *rosea* and the one individual seedling of this variety that was propagated as the clone that was named Rosalind. It was stated that: "Plants of this clone have thus far been incompatible to self- and intra-clonal pollinations. Hence, seeds set by plants of this clone are certain to be from cross-pollinations with other plants, and the seedlings obtained from such plants will not closely resemble the Rosalind Daylily." A report was made of the breeding behavior of Rosalind and of the extent to which it had been used in breeding. In 1938, this clone had already been one of the parents of nearly one-hundred different progenies. It may be stated that this clone is derived from a wild plant, that the clone is diploid (2N:22) and not triploid as is the Europa clone, and that its members have a high degree of potential fertility both as seed and as pollen parents in cross-fertile intra-specific relations with others of the species *H. fulva* and in certain hybridizations with members of other species.

54. Die Gartenzüchtungen der Taglilien. *Gartenschönheit* 19, Juli.

This article was translated into German for this publication by Dr. Camillo Schneider, a well-known botanist and horticulturist. It happened that Dr. Schneider and the writer spent a day together in the summer of 1930 at Wisley, England in the inspection of the collection of *Hemerocallis* in the gardens of the Royal Horticultural Society.

55. What About Daylilies? *Real Gardening* 1:5-11.

56. Hemerocallis. *Monthly Bulletin, The Horticultural Society of New York*, July-September.

This reproduces a photograph of an exhibit of flowers and paintings of *Hemerocallis* and makes the following statement: "Perhaps the most horticulturally outstanding exhibit in the show was the collection of named seedlings and new hybrid selected seedlings of *Hemerocallis*. This 50 square foot group, entered by The New York

Botanical Garden, Bronx Park, N. Y. C., received a Gold Medal, the second to be awarded by the Society this year."

57. The New Boutonniere Daylily. *Horticulture* 16(October 1):380.
58. A Folio of the Genus Hemerocallis. *Bulletin of the Garden Club of America* (1938): 143-44.

    This is the first published memorandum regarding the preparation of a folio with colored plates on the genus *Hemerocallis*. A display of the colored plates was made and a lecture on *Hemerocallis* was given at a meeting of the Garden Club of America.
59. In Memoriam—George Yeld. *Herbertia* 5:61.

    A brief biography of Mr. George Yeld with special mention of his work with *Hemerocallis*.

1939

60. Three New Daylilies. *Journal of the New York Botanical Garden* 40:32-35.

    First descriptions of the clones August Pioneer, Festival, and Hankow. Reprinted in *Garden Digest*, April; and in *The Minnesota Horticulturist*, June.

1940

61. Distributions of the Mikado Daylily. *Journal of the New York Botanical Garden* 41:21.

    With the cooperation of the Farr Nursery Company, which supplied the plants, a total of 258 members of the New York Botanical Garden received one plant each of the Mikado Daylily.
62. William Herbert Medal. *Journal of the New York Botanical Garden* 41:144.

    Mention of the award of this medal by the American Amaryllis Society in recognition of the research done on *Hemerocallis* at the New York Botanical Garden.
63. Arlow Burdette Stout: An Autobiography. *Herbertia* 6(1939):30-40.

    Written in connection with the award of the William Herbert Medal.
64. Newly Named Daylilies. *Herbertia* 6(1939):157-61.
65. Injury to Daylilies by Thrips. *Journal of the New York Botanical Garden* 41:244-45.

The first published account, with photograph, of injuries to daylilies by thrips.

66. Microsporogenesis in Triploid and Diploid Plants of Hemerocallis Fulva. *Bulletin of the Torrey Botanical Club* 67:649-72.

This is a thesis written by Dr. Clyde Chandler who was Technical Assistant at the New York Botanical Garden from 1927 to 1943, during which time Chandler was a valued assistant in the breeding work with *Hemerocallis* and in the cytological studies of this report.

1941

67. Introductions of Daylilies in 1941. *Journal of the New York Botanical Garden* 42:10-17.

Descriptions and photographs of Afterglow, Aladdin, Autumn Prince, Baronet, Bertrand Farr, Bicolor, Brunette, Buckeye, Dominion, Harlequin, Hiawatha, Mignon, Monarch, Port, Red Bird, Sachem, Symphony, Triumph, Yeldrin, and Zouave.

68. The Caballero Daylily. *Journal of the New York Botanical Garden* 42:234.

It was learned that the name Harlequin had already been applied to a daylily and hence the new name Caballero was given to the introduction.

69. Color Patterns in Daylilies. *Journal of the New York Botanical Garden* 42:40-42.

A discussion and classification, with a plate of illustration, of the color patterns in the flowers of daylilies. This plate was republished in *Herbertia* 9 (pl. 233), and again in *Herbertia* 11 (p. 24).

70. Foliage Habits of Daylilies. *Herbertia* 7(1940):156-65.

An account of the dormant, evergreen, and semievergreen habits of growth in species and hybrids of daylilies.

71. Flowering Periods for Clonal varieties of Daylilies. *Herbertia* 7(1940):209-12.

This was written by Miss Selma C. Kojan and was based on observations of the flowering of sixty-four clones of daylilies. The chart that graphically indicates the sequence and the periods of bloom was republished in 1947 in the first *Yearbook of the Midwest Hemerocallis Society* (p. 26). Miss Kojan was Technical Assistant to the writer.

72. The Inflorescence in Hemerocallis. *Bulletin of the Torrey Botanical Club* 68:305-16.

This article explains the structure and methods of the branching in the flower scapes of *Hemerocallis*. The first flowers of the primary inflorescence form a raceme, and in *H. nana* all the flowers are in a simple raceme. In all other of the species now known there are at least some laterals to the flowers of the raceme. A succession of laterals to a flower results in a false axis that appears to be raceme but which is a one-sided cyme that has been called a bostryx. Thus the primary inflorescence is a combination of a raceme and bostryxes. An increase of nodes and segments of a scape below the terminal inflorescence provides for branches from the scape which bear secondary inflorescences. It is the rule that the first flower of a scape to open is the lowermost flower of the primary raceme. Two plates of drawings illustrate all these and other features, such as dichotomous branching and displacement of bracteoles. As a matter of accuracy it may be stated that the writer has never observed any scapes of *Hemerocallis* that were like the scapes shown in the drawing on page 24 of the *Yearbook of The Midwest Hemerocallis Society* for 1947 or on page 24 of the *Yearbook* of 1948.

73. Hybridization and Selective Breeding in the Genus Hemerocallis. *Proceedings of the Seventh International Genetical Congress, Edinburgh, Scotland, August 1939*: 277-78.

1942

74. Foreword. *Herbertia* 8(1941):4-6.
75. Memorandum on a Monograph of the Genus Hemerocallis. *Herbertia* 8(1941):67-71.

    A statement of the character and scope of a proposed monograph with black-and-white reproduction of three of the plates.
76. Report on Intraspecific Hybridizations in Hemerocallis. *Herbertia* 8(1941):95-103.

    A report on the hybridizations that were accomplished at that date.
77. The New Daylilies. *College Bulletin, The Texas State College for Women*, no. 291:15-18.

    Subject matter of an illustrated lecture at Denton, Texas during a garden conference sponsored by Texas Garden Clubs, Inc. and the Texas State College for Women.
78. Daylilies of Chinese Origin. *Journal of the New York Botanical Garden* 43:237-43.

A record and description of the different daylilies obtained from China and of their use in breeding.

79. The Horticultural Development of Daylilies. *Home Gardening* (New Orleans) 3, November.

1943

80. *Hemerocallis altissima* Stout, sp. nov. *Herbertia* 9(1942):103-6.

Original description of this species with photographs of a plant, flowers, and roots.

81. Origin and Genetics of Some Classes of Red-flowered Daylilies. *Herbertia* 9(1942):161-74.

This has the first publication of the plate showing the ancestry of the Theron Daylily. There was also a republication of the plate showing color patterns and of the plate showing flowers of wild fulvous daylilies.

1944

82. The Elmer A. Claar Daylily. *Herbertia* 10(1943):76-78.

Description and photograph of flowers of this daylily and of the Festival Daylily.

83. Concerning Injury to Daylilies by Thrips. *Herbertia* 10(1943):176-79.

1945

84. Daylilies: Old and New. *Monthly Bulletin, Horticultural Society of New York* 16:7-9.

A summary of the subject matter of a lecture to the Horticultural Society of New York. A lecture on daylilies, with various treatments of the subject and with profuse illustrations by lantern slides, has been presented on numerous occasions rather widely in the United States and once in Scotland at the Royal Botanical Gardens in Edinburgh.

1946

85. The Synflorescence of Amaryllis Hybrids. *Herbertia* 11(1944):268-73.

Includes drawings and a description of a typical synflorescence of *Hemerocallis middendorffii*.

86. The Quilled-Petal Character in Daylilies. *Herbertia* 11(1944):307-8.

87. Introductions of Daylilies in 1946. *Journal of the New York Botanical Garden* 47: 77-82.

First descriptions of the clones August Orange, Blanche Hooker, Caprice, Fantasia, Fiftieth Anniversary, Firebrand, Georgia, Manchu, Rose Gem, and Viking.

88. Types of Anthesis in Hemerocallis and their Heredity in F_1 Hybrids. *Bulletin of the Torrey Botanical Club* 73:134-54.

An explanation and discussion of diurnal, nocturnal, and extended types of the flowering of daylilies and of the flowering behavior of hybrids. These are indicated graphically by means of anthograms.

1947

89. The Character and Genetics of Doubleness in the Flowers of Daylilies: The Para-Double Class. *Herbertia* 12(1945):113-23.

This explains and illustrates the character of the flowers in the Flore Pleno and Kwanso clones. Data on the genetics of the para-double class are reported. There are illustrations of the two-, the three-, and the four-bladed petaloids that occur in the flowers of these two clones. In a flower of the para-double type there are three sepals and three petals in the first two whorls of the flower. The doubleness consists of additional whorls of stamens and petaloids and the pistil is absent or abnormal. The semi-double type of flower has, usually, no increase in the number of flower parts but stamens are transformed into petaloids. The pseudo-double type of flower (as shown in the *Yearbook of the Midwest Hemerocallis Society*, 1948: 2) has an additional segment without an increase of whorls. Frequently there are four sepals, four petals, and four stamens in each of the two whorls. The increase in the members of each whorl may continue until there is a fasciation of two flowers. This type of flower is sporadic and fluctuating in daylilies.

90. Daylilies at the Garden. *Through the Garden Gate* 2 (no. 3).

An account of the daylilies to be seen at the New York Botanical Garden.

91. Daylilies: Old and New. *Yearbook of the Midwest Hemerocallis Society*, 1947: 27-30.

Has photos of the flowers of Festival, Mikado, Summer Multiflava Hybrids, Taruga, Theron, and Vesta.

92. The Theron Daylily. *Yearbook of the Midwest Hemerocallis Society*, 1947: 57-58.

An account of the results of selective breeding for different classes of red-flowered daylilies with special mention of the intensification of anthocyanin pigment seen in the Theron class.

1948

93. Daylily. *Taylor's Encyclopedia of Gardening*, 2d ed. Boston: American Garden Guild, 280-81.

Revised list of the most important species of *Hemerocallis* and of horticultural clones, with discussions of their culture and propagation.

94. The Europa Daylily. *Flower Grower* 35 (no. 7).

An account of the "round-the-world trail" of this clone with six illustrations.

95. A New Race of Double-Flowered Daylilies. *Journal of the New York Botanical Garden* 49:236-38.

This illustrates and describes the flowers of a semi-double type of flower obtained after about twenty years of selective breeding.

1949

96. Daylilies Being Introduced in 1949. *Journal of the New York Botanical Garden* 50:36-39.

Descriptions, with illustrations, of the Elfin Daylilies and the clones Cathay, Challenger, Red Knight, Red Lady, and Ming.

97. The Tall Daylilies. *Yearbook of the Midwest Hemerocallis Society*, 1948:59-66.

Data on the genetics of hybridizations involving *Hemerocallis citrina* and *H. exaltata* are given, with several photographs.

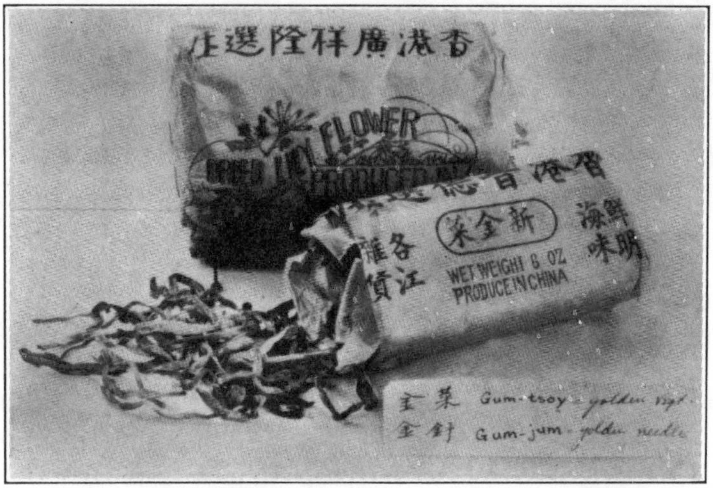

Plate 34. Pound and half-pound packages of gum-jum imported for sale in New York City

Plate 35. Plant of *H. fulva*, showing fleshy roots and rhizomes

APPENDIX C

A SELECTION OF HEMEROCALLIS LITERATURE SUBSEQUENT TO THE PUBLICATION OF A. B. STOUT'S *DAYLILIES* IN 1934

1. Darrow, George M., and Frederick G. Meyer, eds. *Daylily Handbook. The American Horticulture Magazine* 47, no. 2 (1968).
2. Davis, Ben Arthur. *Daylilies and How to Grow Them.* Atlanta: Tupper & Love, 1954.
3. Stuntz, F. M., et al. *Hemerocallis Check List 1893 to July 1, 1957.* American Hemerocallis Society, Inc., 1957.
4. Monroe, W. E. *Hemerocallis Check List July 1, 1957 to July 1, 1973.* American Hemerocallis Society, Inc., 1973.
5. — *Hemerocallis Check List July 1, 1973 to December 31, 1983.* American Hemerocallis Society, Inc., 1983.
6. Traub, H. P. Colchicine-induced Hemerocallis Polyploids and Their Breeding Behavior. *Plant Life* 7 (1951): 83-116.
7. Hu, Shiu-Ying. An Early History of Daylily. *Daylily Handbook. The American Horticulture Magazine* 47, no. 2 (1968): 51-85.
8. Asen, S., and T. Arisumi. Anthocyanins from Hemerocallis. *Proceedings of the American Society of Horticulture Science* 92 (1968): 641-45.
9. Bisset, K. Hemerocallis Pigments. Ph.D. diss., Institute of Molecular Biophysics, Florida State University, Tallahassee, 1976.
10. Heuser, C. W., and D. A. Apps. In Vitro Plantlet Formation from Flower Petal Explants of Hemerocallis cv. Chipper Cherry. *Canadian Journal of Botany* 54 (1976): 616-18.

Plate 36. Habits of growth. (1) *H. Dumortierii*; (2) *H. citrina*; (3) *H. Middendorffii*

APPENDIX D

DAYLILY SOURCES

The following list has been adapted from one furnished by the American Hemerocallis Society and another prepared by Richard Kitchingman for the British Hosta and Hemerocallis Society. The lists were current for 1985. Daylily price lists or catalogs should be available from most of these sources on request, though in some cases there is a small charge to cover the cost of mailing.

As of March 1986, the address of the American Hemerocallis Society is c/o Ainie Busse, secretary, Route 2, Box 13, Cokato, Minnesota 55321. The British Hosta and Hemerocallis Society can be contacted c/o R.M. Kitchingman, honorary secretary, Garden Cottage, St. Andrew's School, Horsell, Woking, GU21 4QW, England.

USA

Alabama

Bush Gardens, Route 1, Box 115, Headland, Alabama 36345
Hill Top Garden, Route 5, Box 65, Hamilton, Alabama 35570
Jedi Daylily Garden, 100 Ray Street, Flomaton, Alabama 36441
Jimmie's Gardens, Route 1, Box 173, Berry, Alabama 35546
Mayo's Daylilies, Route 2, Box 255, Reform, Alabama 35481
Pate Daylily Garden, Route 2, Box 328, Altoona, Alabama 35952
Pierce Daylily Garden, 2361 East Road, Mobile, Alabama 36609

California

Alpine Valley Gardens, 2627 Calistoga Road, Santa Rosa, California 95404
Cordon Bleu Farms, P.O. Box 2033, San Marcos, California 92069
Greenwood Nursery, 2 El Camino Réal, Goleta, California 93117

Iris Lane Gardens, 1649 S. Iris Lane, Escondido, California 92026
Melrose Gardens, 309 Best Road South, Stockton, California 95205

Connecticut

Lee Bristol Nursery, P.O. Box 5, Gaylordsville, Connecticut 06755
White Flower Farm, Litchfield, Connecticut 06759

Florida

Big Tree Daylily Garden, 777 General Hutchinson Parkway, Longwood, Florida 32750
Corner Oaks Garden, 6139 Blanding Boulevard, Jacksonville, Florida 32214
Daylily World, P.O. Box 1612, Sanford, Florida 32771
Hemer Heaven, P.O. Box 18017, Orlando, Florida 32860
Ladybug Beautiful Gardens, 857 Leopard Trail, Winter Springs, Florida 32708
Lena's Daylilies, 1635 Atwood Drive, Pensacola, Florida 32514
Jeff and Elizabeth Salter, 1471 Lancelot Way, Casselberry, Florida 32707
Solano Grove Gardens, Route 2, Box 367-D, St. Augustine, Florida 32084
Stateler's Flower Farm, P.O. Box 27, Loughman, Florida 33858
Wimberlyway Gardens, 7024 N.W. 18th Avenue, Gainesville, Florida 32605

Georgia

Damascus Gardens, 4454 Francis Court, Lilburn, Georgia 30247
Hendricks Daylily Garden, P.O. Box 86, Woodland, Georgia 31836
JB-2 Gardens and Gifts, 8601 Creighton Place West, Savannah, Georgia 31406
Lily Bend Nursery Company, Route 2, Box 254-E, Valdosta, Georgia 31601
One Horse Farm and Gardens, 186 Sandefur Road, Kathleen, Georgia 31047
Thomasville Nurseries, P.O. Box 7, Thomasville, Georgia 31792-

Illinois

The Flower Ladies Garden, 1560 Johnson Road, Granite City, Illinois 62040

Illini Iris, Route 1, Box 5, N. State Street Road, Monticello, Illinois 61856

Klehm's Nursery, Route 5, Box 197, Barrington, Illinois 60010

Indiana

Anderson's Daylily Garden, 7909 Placing Road, Indianapolis, Indiana 46226

Breezy Hill Garden, 7460 Burr Street, Merrillville, Indiana, 46410

Coburg Planting Fields, 573 E. 600 North, Valparaiso, Indiana 46383

Shields Horticultural Gardens, P.O. Box 92, Westfield, Indiana 46074

Soules Garden, 5809 Rahke Road, Indianapolis, Indiana 46217

Kansas

Schoonover Gardens, 404 South 5th, Humboldt, Kansas 66748

Louisiana

Patsy Ruth Alford, Route 3, Box 99, Marion, Louisiana 71260

Beckham's Garden (Amarylis, Inc.), 1452 Glenmore Avenue, Baton Rouge, Louisiana 70808

Crochet Daylily Garden, P.O. Box 425, Prairieville, Louisiana 70769

Fenton Daylily Garden, P.O. Box 141, Fenton, Louisiana 70640

Guidry's Daylily Garden, 1005 E. Vermilion, Abbeville, Louisiana 70510

Hobby Garden, 38164 Monticello Drive, Prairieville, Louisiana 70769

Louisiana Nursery, Route 7, Box 43, Opelousas, Louisiana 70570

Maggie's Daylily Garden, 100 Rosewood Drive, Hammond, Louisiana 70401

Tanner's Garden, Route 1, Box 22, Cheneyville, Louisiana 71325

Maine

Four Winds Garden, P.O. Box 141, South Harpswell, Maine 04079

Hermitage Gardens, RFD 1, Box 106, Monroe, Maine 04951

Maryland

Frank L. Bennett, 21621 Second Street, Laytonsville, Maryland 20879
Peters Starmont Daylilies, 10111 Norton Road, Potomac, Maryland 20854
Ridge Iris and Daylily Gardens, 7314 Ridge Road, Hanover, Maryland 21076
Webber Gardens, 9180 Main Street, Damascus, Maryland 20872

Massachusetts

Seawright Gardens, 134 Indian Hill, Carlisle, Massachusetts 01714
Tranquil Lake Nursery, 45 River Street, Rehoboth, Massachusetts 02769

Michigan

Englerth Gardens, 2461 22nd Street, Hopkins, Michigan 49328
Hite Garden, 370 Gallogly Road, Pontiac, Michigan 48055

Minnesota

Borbeleta Gardens, 10078 154th Avenue, Elk River, Minnesota 55330-6233
Busse Gardens, Route 2, Box 13, Cokato, Minnesota 55321
Fairway Hosta Gardens, 114 The Fairway, Albert Lea, Minnesota 56007

Mississippi

Sullivan's Garden, 2813 North 7th Avenue, Laurel, Mississippi 39440

Missouri

Frank A. Kropf, Route 2, Box 127, Mexico, Missouri 65265
Lenington Long Gardens, 7007 Manchester Road, Kansas City, Missouri 64133
River City Daylilies, 779 Perry Avenue, Cape Girardeau, Missouri 63701
Stewart P. Smith (Mr. and Mrs.), 501 Bourn Avenue, Columbia, Missouri 65203
Gilbert H. Wild & Son, Inc., 1112 Joplin Street, Sarcoxie, Missouri 64862-0338

New York

Richard J. Bennett, 1196 Long Pond Road, Rochester, New York 14626
Floyd Cove Nursery, 11 Shipyard Lane, Setauket, New York 11733
Saxton Gardens, 1 First Street, Saratoga Springs, New York 12866
John Scheepers, 63 Wall Street, New York, New York 10005

North Carolina

Harold H. Kirk, 200 Knollwood Drive, Morganton, North Carolina 28655
Lake Norman Gardens, P.O. Box 1617, Davidson, North Carolina 28036
Oxford Gardens, 3022 Oxford Drive, Durham, North Carolina 27707
Powell's Gardens, Route 2, Box 86, Princeton, North Carolina, 27569

Ohio

Moldovan's Gardens, 38830 Detroit Road, Avon, Ohio 44011

Oregon

Caprice Farm Nursery, 15425 S. Pleasant Hill Road, Sherwood, Oregon 97140
Pilley's Garden, 2829 Favill Lane, Grant's Pass, Oregon 97526

Pennsylvania

Boylan Gardens, Route 1, Venango Avenue, Cambridge Springs, Pennsylvania 16403
Hickory Hill Gardens, R.D. 1, Box 11, Loretto, Pennsylvania 15940

South Carolina

Meadowlake Gardens, Route 4, Box 709, Walterboro, South Carolina 29488
Meadow Rose, P.O. Box 1041, Clemson, South Carolina 29633
Velerie P. Rushing, 823 Boundary Street, Newberry, South Carolina 29108
Wayside Gardens, Hodges, South Carolina 29695

Tennessee

Oakes Daylilies, Route 3, Corryton, Tennessee 37721
Scott Daylily Farm, 5830 Clark Road, Harrison, Tennessee 37341

Texas

Ater Daylilies, 3803 Greystone Drive, Austin, Texas 78731
Barnee's Garden, Route 10, Box 2010, Nacogdoches, Texas 75961
Bluebird Sands, Route 1, Box 78, Murchison, Texas 75778
Albert C. Faggard, 3840 Le Bleu Street, Beaumont, Texas 77707
Glidden Gardens, 714 Benbrook, Houston, Texas 77706
Houston Daylily Gardens, Inc., P.O. Box 7008, The Woodlands, Texas 77380
Hughes Garden, 2450 North Main Street, Mansfield, Texas 76063
Tarrant Daylily Garden, Route 1, 7135 Highway 36, Freeport, Texas 77541

Virginia

Branham Farms, Ltd., 607 Woodhaven Drive, Richmond, Virginia 23224
Samar, 408 Riverside Drive, Fredericksburg, Virginia 22401
Solomon Daylilies, 105 Country Club Road, Newport News, Virginia 23606

Washington

Donna's Lilies of the Valley, 1221 Highway 7 N., Tonasket, Washington 98855

ENGLAND

Ballalheannagh Nurseries, Glen Roy, Loanan, Isle of Man
Banwell Nurseries, Banwell, Avon
Roger Bowden, Cleave House, Sticklepath, Devon
Bressingham Gardens, Diss, Norfolk
Broadleigh Gardens, Bishop's Hull, Taunton, Somerset
Bullwood Nursery, 54 Woodland Avenue, Hockley, Essex
Caldwell's Nurseries, Chelford Road, Knutsford, Cheshire
Carlisle's Ltd., Loddon Nurseries, Twyford, Berks
D. J. Case, Higher End Nursery, Fordingbridge, Hants

Peter Chapell, Spinners, Boldre, Hants
Churchills Nurseries, Chudleigh, Devon
Coomblands Nurseries, Leavesden, Watford, Herts
County Park Nurseries, Essex Gardens, Hornchurch, Essex
Everton Nurseries, Everton, Hants
The Floreat Gardens, 148 Albert Road, Parkstone, Dorset
William Fuller & Son, Little Woodcote Lane, Purley, Surrey
Garden House Farm, Drinkstone, Bury St. Edmunds, Suffolk IP30 9TN
Great Dixter Nurseries, Northiam, Surrey
Growing Carpets, Royston, Herts
Hadspen House Nursery, Castle Combe, Somerset
Higher End Nurseries, Fordingbridge, Hants
Hilliers Nurseries, Romsey Road, Winchester, Hants
Holden Clough Nurseries, Bolton-by-Bowland, Clitheroe, Lancs
Hopley's Plants, High Street, Much Hadham, Herts
Hydon Nurseries, Clockbarn Lane, Hydon Heath, Godalming, Surrey
Jackamoor Hardy Plant Farm, Theobald Park Road, Enfield, Middx
Reginald Kaye, Waithman Nurseries, Silverdale, Carnforth, Lancs
Kelways, The Royal Nurseries, Langport, Somerset TA10 9SH
Mallorn Gardens, Carn View, Lanner Hill, Redruth, Cornwall
Mears Close Nurseries, Tadworth Street, Tadworth, Surrey
Norton Hall Daylilies, 7 Hillyard Road, London, W7 IBH
Paradise Centre, Twinstead Road, Lamarsh, Bures, Suffolk, CO8 5EX
J. Parker Ltd., Spalding, Lincs
J. E. Parker-Jervis, Marten's Hall Farm, Longworth, Abingdon, Oxon
Perryhill Nurseries, Hartfield, Sussex
Plants for Pleasure, 2 The Cottage, Maybourne Rise, Mayford, Surrey
Robinsons Gardens, Knockholt, Sevenoaks, Kent
Robinsons Hardy Plants, Crockenhall, Swanley, Kent
Rougham Hall Nurseries, Ipswich Road, Rougham, Suffolk, IP30 9L2
L. R. Russell Nurseries, Windlesham, Surrey
St. Bridget Nurseries, Taunton, Somerset
Sawley Nursery, Risplith, Ripon, Yorks
John Scott's Nurseries, Merriott, Somerset
Stapeley Water Gardens, 92 London Road, Stapeley, Nantwich, Cheshire
Sunningdale Nurseries, Windlesham, Surrey

F. Toynbee Ltd., Croftway Nurseries, Barnham, Bognor Regis, Sussex
Treasures Ltd., Burford House, Tenbury Wells, Worcs
Unusual Plants, White Barn House, Elmstead Market, Colchester, Essex
The Variegated Garden, 5 Rockley Avenue, Radcliffe-on-Trent, Notts
R. Veitch & Sons, The Royal Nurseries, Alphington, Exeter, Devon
Wallace and Barr Ltd., The Nurseries, Marden, Kent
White Barn House, Elmstead Market, Colchester, Essex

SCOTLAND

The Gardens Nursery, Dunnichen, Forfar, Angus

FRANCE

Michele Bourdillion, 41230 Mur de Sologne, Soings-en-Sologne
Jean Cayeaux, Poilly-les-Gien, 45500 Gien, Loiret

BELGIUM

R. Ignace van Dorslaer, 12 Kapellan Dries, 93.31 Melle Gerstrode
Jardinaart van Mulders, Meerstraat 11, B 3020 Wijgmaal

THE NETHERLANDS

C. W. Jansen, Kievitsbloem 27, 7721 HK Dalfsen
S. J. Spyree, B. V. Weiresteen Straat 144, 2181 6D Hillegom

WEST GERMANY

Walter Erhardt, 8651 Langenstadt 64
Kaiser and Siebert, 6101 Rossdorf bei Darmstadt
Heinz Klose, Rosenstrasse 10, 3503 Loehfeldon-bei-Kassel
Werner Reinemann, Burgerweg 8, 4437 Schöppingen
Dr. Hans Simon, Gartnerischer Pflanzenbau, D8772 Marktheidenfeld
Staudgartneret von Zeppelin, D7811 Salzburg-Laufen

EAST GERMANY

Eberhard Schuster, Gartenbaubetries, Post Gadebehn, 2711 Augostenhof

APPENDIX E

DAYLILY CULTIVARS THAT HAVE RECEIVED THE STOUT MEDAL OF THE AMERICAN HEMEROCALLIS SOCIETY

Year	*Cultivar*	*Breeder*
1950	Hesperus	H. P. Sass
1951	Painted Lady	Russell
1952	Potentate	Nesmith
1953	Revolute	H. P. Sass
1954	Dauntless	Stout
1955	Prima Donna	Taylor
1956	Naranja	Wheeler
1957	Ruffled Pinafore	Millikan
1958	High Noon	Millikan
1959	Salmon Sheen	Taylor
1960	Fairy Wings	Lester
1961	Playboy	Wheeler
1962	Bess Ross	Claar
1963	Multnomah	Kraus
1964	Frances Fay	Fay
1965	Luxury Lace	E. Spalding
1966	Cartwheels	Fay
1967	Full Reward	McVicker
1968	Satin Glass	Fay-Hardy
1969	May Hall	Hall
1970	Ava Michelle	Flory
1971	Renee	Dill
1972	Hortensia	Branch
1973	Lavender Flight	E. Spalding
1974	Winning Ways	Wild
1975	Clarence Simon	MacMillan
1976	Green Flutter	L. Williamson

1977	Green Glitter	D. J. Harrison
1978	Mary Todd	Fay
1979	Moment of Truth	MacMillan
1980	Bertie Ferris	Winniford
1981	Ed Murray	Grovatt
1982	Ruffled Apricot	S. H. Baker
1983	Sabie	MacMillan
1984	My Belle	Durio
1985	Stella de Oro	Jablonski

INDEX

The special discussion of a subject begins on the page that is printed in **bold face** type. Illustration in plates is indicated by *italics*.